A New Owner's
GUIDE TO
Samoyeds

Terry & Gail Campbell

Overleaf: A Samoyed adult and puppy photographed by Isabelle Francais.

Opposite page: A Samoyed owned by David and Bonnie Prell.

The publisher wishes to acknowledge the following owners of the dogs in this book: Ala-Kasam Samoyeds, Barbara Brisgel, Terry and Gail Campbell, Barbara Cole, J. Feinberg, Donna Marie Freudig, Joan Froling, Ken Granacki, Debbie Haynes, Donald and Dot Hodges, Patty Koontz, Anne O'Neill, David and Bonnie Prell, Dianne Sorrentino, Charles Ward.

Photographers: Paulette Braun, Warren Cook, Daniels Studio, Isabelle Francais, Garden Studios, Kitten Rodwell, Inc., MikRon Photos, Robert Pearcy, Vince Serbin, Judith Strom, Karen Taylor.

The author acknowledges the contribution of Judy Iby for the following chapters: Sport of Purebred Dogs, Identification and Finding the Lost Dog, Traveling with Your Dog, Behavior and Canine Communication, and Health Care.

The portrayal of canine pet products in this book is for general instructive value only; the appearance of such products does not necessarily constitute an endorsement by the authors, the publisher, or the owners of the dogs portrayed in this book.

© T.F.H. Publications, Inc.

Distributed in the UNITED STATES to the Pet Trade by T.F.H. Publications, Inc., One T.F.H. Plaza, Neptune City, NJ 07753; distributed in the UNITED STATES to the Bookstore and Library Trade by National Book Network, Inc. 4720 Boston Way, Lanham MD 20706; in CANADA to the Pet Trade by H & L Pet Supplies Inc., 27 Kingston Crescent, Kitchener, Ontario N2B 2T6; Rolf C. Hagen Inc., 3225 Sartelon St. Laurent-Montreal Quebec H4R 1E8; in CANADA to the Book Trade by Vanwell Publishing Ltd., 1 Northrup Crescent, St. Catharines, Ontario L2M 6P5 ; in ENGLAND by T.F.H. Publications, PO Box 15, Waterlooville PO7 6BQ; in AUSTRALIA AND THE SOUTH PACIFIC by T.F.H. (Australia), Pty. Ltd., Box 149, Brookvale 2100 N.S.W., Australia; in NEW ZEALAND by Brooklands Aquarium Ltd. 5 McGiven Drive, New Plymouth, RD1 New Zealand; in Japan by T.F.H. Publications, Japan—Jiro Tsuda, 10-12-3 Ohjidai, Sakura, Chiba 285, Japan; in SOUTH AFRICA by Lopis (Pty) Ltd., P.O. Box 39127, Booysens, 2016, Johannesburg, South Africa. Published by T.F.H. Publications, Inc.
MANUFACTURED IN THE
UNITED STATES OF AMERICA
BY T.F.H. PUBLICATIONS, INC.

A New Owner's
Guide to
Samoyeds

Terry & Gail Campbell

Contents

It's hard to resist a sweet Sammy puppy!

The Samoyed's beautiful, weather-resistant coat makes him perfect for outdoor activities.

The Samoyed makes a wonderful companion for the whole family.

The Samoyed is a working dog that is very graceful and athletic.

The versatile Samoyed can participate in many events.

HISTORY of the Samoyed

As civilization dawned on the world over 10,000 years ago, a strange but symbiotic relationship had already begun to establish itself between early man and one of the beasts of the forest. Man's pursuits at that time, were primarily involved with providing food for himself and his family and protecting the members of his tribe from always present danger.

In doing so, man undoubtedly saw his own survival efforts reflected in the habits of the beast that made ever-increasing overtures at coexistence. That beast was none other than *Canis lupis*—the wolf.

One of the most versatile of all breeds, the Samoyed can be a well-mannered house dog as well as a rough-and-ready outdoorsman.

The transition from wolf-in-the-wild to "man's best friend," *Canis familiaris*, is a tale as long and fascinating as it is fraught with widely varying explanations. However, it seems obvious that observation of the wolf could easily have taught early man some effective hunting skills that he too would be able to use advantageously. Wolves saw a source of easily secured food in man's discards. The association grew from there.

It became increasingly obvious as the man-wolf relationship developed through the ages, that certain descendants of these increasingly domesticated wolves could also be used by man to assist in many of his survival pursuits. The wolves that could assist man in satisfying the unending human need for food were of course most highly prized.

These wolves-cum-dogs were not only capable of deciding which game was most apt to be easy prey, they knew how to separate the chosen animal from the herd and also how to bring it to ground. These abilities did not escape the notice of man.

Richard and Alice Feinnes, authors of *The Natural History of Dogs*, classify most dogs as having descended from one of

four major groups: the Dingo group, the Greyhound group, the Mastiff group and the Northern or Arctic group. Each of these groups trace back to separate and distinct branches of the wolf family.

The Dingo group traces its origin to the Asian wolf (*Canis lupis pallipes*). The Greyhound group also descends from a coursing type relative of the Asian wolf. The Mastiff group owes its primary heritage to the Tibetan wolf (*Canis lupis chanco* or *laniger*). The great diversity of the dogs included in this group indicate they are not entirely of pure blood in that the specific breeds included have undoubtedly been influenced by descendants of the other three groups.

The fourth classification is the Arctic or Nordic group of dogs which is a direct descendent of the rugged northern wolf (*Canis lupis*). Included in the many breeds of this group are: the Alaskan Malamute, Chow Chow, German Shepherd, the much smaller Welsh Corgi and Spitz type dogs and the Samoyede.

The Northern group, like their undomesticated ancestors, maintained the characteristics that

It is important to remember that the Samoyed's heritage includes a history as a herding dog. Spirit, owned by Debbie Haynes, calls upon this ability to herd sheep.

Samoyeds are working dogs and have a natural instinct for sledding. This pair is harnessed and ready to go.

protect them from the harsh environment of the upper European countries. Weather resistant coats were of the ideal texture to protect from rain and cold. There was a long coarse outercoat that shed snow and rain and a dense undercoat that insulated against subzero temperatures. These coats were especially abundant around the neck and chest and thereby offered double protection for the vital organs.

Well-coated tails could cover and protect the nose and mouth should the animal be forced to sleep in the snow. Small prick ears were not as easily frostbitten or frozen as the large and pendulous ear of some of the other breeds. The muzzle had sufficient length to warm the frigid air before it reached the lungs. Leg length was sufficient to keep the chest and abdomen above the snow line. Tails were carried horizontally or up over the back rather than trailing behind in the snow.

Skeletal remains of these early wolf descendants have been

found throughout Northern and Central Europe, northern Asia and the Arctic regions of North America. The group stands as the forerunner of what are also commonly referred to as the Arctic breeds.

The Arctic group itself can be divided into four categories: hunting dogs (examples: Norwegian Elkhound, Chow Chow and Karelian Bear Dog), draft dogs (Alaskan Malamute, Siberian Husky), herding dogs (Samoyede, Swedish and Finnish Lapphunds) and companion dogs (including most of the Spitz type dogs—German Spitz, Japanese Spitz, American Eskimo and Volpino Italiano).

This is not to indicate that there were no cross-breedings of the types nor that abilities peculiar to one group may not have also have been possessed by another. In fact, some historians believe that many of the Northern or Arctic breeds that retain a degree of hunting ability owe this strength to their Asian Dingo-type heritage that is absent from other breeds whose ancestors were not exposed to this admixture. It is also believed that this cross provided some of these Northern breeds with a more refined attitude and tractability. There is little doubt that the Samoyede qualifies to be placed in this category.

The Samoyede breed was developed during the reign of the Russian Czars by the ancient tribe of people whose descendants lived in the tundra region reaching from North Central Siberia to Northern Europe. These people are credited for developing their dogs not simply as sled dogs of great note but as all-around assistants to man.

The incredibly rugged constitution of this particular family of dogs was inherited from their northern wolf ancestors. The ruggedness made the dogs as valuable to man as the other breeds that were "tamed" well enough to serve as drought dogs, but the Samoyede tribes' dogs had a distinct advantage as well. Through selection the tribes people had developed their breed of dog so that it also served as herder, hunter, guard and companion. The roles of guard and companion being of particular importance in that the tractability of their breed even permitted the dogs into their owners' living quarters. The breed lived closely with its people and this is why it is believed that the modern Samoyede is such a people-oriented breed—residing happily indoors or out.

The inaccessibility of the regions that the Samoyede tribes had occupied resulted in their dogs being recognized as one of the oldest and purest breeds known to man. "Purest" in the sense that no admixture of other breeds or crossbacks to their lupine ancestors were used once the breed was established.

Because of its Northern heritage and the many characteristics which identify that heritage, Samoyedes are mistakenly classified simply as another breed of sled dog. Quite the opposite is true. The historic versatility of this breed is not only documented by "outsiders," i.e., historians and sled dog enthusiasts, it is unquestionably confirmed by such noted Samoyede authorities as Mrs. Ivy Kilburn Morris (the former Ivy Kilburn Scott). The late Mrs. Kilburn Morris was daughter of Ernest Kilburn Scott, original importer of Samoyedes to England who wrote the first standard of the breed.

Mrs. Scott lived out her later years in Durban, South Africa and it was there, in a historical meeting with Richard

Through rain, sleet or snow (or lack of it!), this Samoyed team demonstrates not only their competency but their joy at performing at a weight pull competition.

Beauchamp in 1984, that she spoke long and eloquently of the history and use of the dogs her father had first brought to England.

"Some were almost brown when they arrived," she said. "Partly because they were a biscuit-cream sort of a color and partly because they had never seen a soap bath in their lives. The dogs were used as many things in Archangel (Russia) where my father first got his, but I want to state emphatically that the Samoyede is not simply a sledge dog! Any breed can pull a sledge." She went on to state that it was wrong to say the breed was "just any one thing" but if it were necessary to do so, "they should be classified as herding dogs."

The breed first became recognized by the western world when Fridtjof Nansen, the Norwegian explorer, relied on teams of Samoyedes during his 1894 expedition to the North Pole. Nansen's glowing reports and recommendation brought the Samoyede dogs to the attention of other explorers. The Arctic explorers following Nansen employed the services of the Samoyede with varying degrees of success. However, more often than not, when the dogs did not achieve the goals set for them by their explorer-owners, failure was due far more to human error rather than canine inability.

THE SAMOYED IN ENGLAND

The first Samoyede dog to be imported into England as a foundation dog for a breeding program was Sabarka, a brown colored dog with a white chest and feet. Sabarka was purchased in 1889 in Archangel, Russia by Ernest Kilburn Scott as a gift for his wife. The breed's color varied from tribe to tribe but it was the beautiful white dogs seen in his expeditions that caught the eye of Kilburn Scott. Soon after, the Kilburn Scotts imported Whitey Petchora, a cream colored female. The two imports were bred together and offspring found their way into the hands of other English dog lovers who championed the cause of the beautiful Arctic dogs.

During the following few decades the number of imports and homebreds grew. The breed was given the name "Samoyede" by Kilburn Scott in 1892 but that designation did not become official until 1909.

The breed was first shown at the Leeds Dog Show in 1893 in the Foreign Dog Class as "Samozia Sledge Dogs." It was not until 1901 that The Kennel Club in England granted the breed registration privileges. Full breed recognition came in 1909. In that same year the Kilburn Scotts' designation of the breed as the "Samoyede" was given official sanction (later the final "e" was dropped) along with a standard of the breed which also had been drawn up by the Kilburn Scotts.

The Samoyede Club was formed in that year as well but the club was for male owners exclusively. The ladies formed their own club three years later and the two organizations operated independently until 1920 when the they merged to form the Samoyed Association of Great Britain. Major Frederick Jackson served as president of the combined club until he died in 1938.

Samoyeds have an uncanny ability to reflect the moods of their loved ones. A happy owner makes a happy Sammy!

THE SAMOYED COMES TO AMERICA

In 1902 Mercy d'Argenteau, the Princess de Montyglyon, a Belgian Countess and hereditary Princess of the Holy Roman Empire, journeyed to St. Petersburg, Russia. The Princess was an ardent dog fancier and while in St. Petersburg attended the dog show held in that city.

There she saw and fell in love with a large white Russian champion Samoyed dog named Moustan. Moustan had been entered at the show by his owner the Grand Duke Michael, brother of Czar Nicholas II. In the truly grand tradition of the Russian Monarchy, Duke Michael gave the Princess the dog as a gift.

This ignited the Princess's interest in the breed so much that by 1904 when she immigrated to the United States she was accompanied not only by Mouston but three other Samoyeds as well. Moustan was shown extensively and in 1906 became the first of his breed to be registered with the American Kennel Club.

Without-a-doubt, World War I had severe impact on the Samoyed both here and abroad. However, as peace returned, there was a definite upswing in breed interest. Imports continued and notable fanciers were attracted to the Samoyed.

Mr. & Mrs. Alfred H. Seeley were said to have made the greatest contribution to the Samoyed breed in America by importing dogs from England that descended directly from the most famous Siberian and Arctic expeditionary stock.

An interesting tale was recounted by Mr. Seeley regarding the use of Samoyeds during a polar expedition from England around the turn of the century. He said some members of the expedition mistakenly advocated docking the dogs' tails in that the tails, "interfered to some degree with the dogs' speed."

The dogs all died of pneumonia very shortly in that they were robbed of the ability to use their tails as covers for their muzzles when sleeping in the open. Thus it was realized the tails acted as filters to warm the frigid air before it entered the lungs.

The Samoyed's loving smile and happy expression demonstrate two attributes of his personality.

In 1923, The Samoyed Club of America was formed in New York City. The English breed standard was adopted in full but according to Robert H. and Dolly Ward's *The Complete Samoyed*, the words, "black or black spots to disqualify" were added.

The organization held its first parent club specialty show in 1929 in conjunction with the Tuxedo Kennel Club Dog Show. There was an entry of 40 dogs.

As the years progressed through the 30s and 40s, the Samoyed breed grew in numbers and strength placing in and winning Working Groups throughout the country. Following the years of World War II, enthusiasm leapt forward and in 1949 the breed achieved its ultimate recognition by winning Best in Show at the Toledo Kennel Club's all-breed show in Toledo, Ohio. The winner of this historic award was Sweet Missy of Sammar, a beautiful bitch owned by Mr. & Mrs. J. J. Marshall, Jr. She came up from the puppy class to top the Breed and Working Group under breeder-judge, Mrs. Anastasia MacBain. Mrs. Marie Meyer presented the Best in Show award.

Can. Am. Ch. Bykhal's Northern Exposure, owned by David and Bonnie Prell, is all set to participate in a backpacking event, where the dog carries his own food, water and supplies.

CHARACTERISTICS of the Samoyed

If you are still in the "deciding" stage of whether or not you should bring a Samoyed puppy into your life, we caution that you do not, and we repeat do not, visit a kennel or home in which there are Sammy puppies. You will find it next to impossible to leave without one! Sammy puppies are absolutely irresistible! Of all the breeds we have known in our lives, none is more captivating than these little snowballs of personality.

It is for this very reason that the person anticipating owning a Samoyed give serious thought to the decision. All puppies are picture-postcard cuddly and cute, Samoyed puppies particularly so. There is nothing more seductive than a litter of fluffy little puppies, nestled together sound asleep, one on top of the other. In addition to being cute, puppies are living,

Truly a breed for all seasons, the Samoyed's coat protects him from freezing temperatures and icy waters.

breathing and very mischievous little creatures and they are entirely dependent upon their human owner for everything once they leave their mother and littermates. Further, the fluffy and dependent puppy quickly becomes a bundle of activity with adolescent hormones continuously raging and inspiring relentless activity.

Buying a dog, especially a puppy, before someone is absolutely sure they want to make that commitment can be a serious mistake. The prospective dog owner must clearly understand the amount of time and work involved in dog ownership. Failure to understand the extent of commitment

Sammy puppies are irresistible! This sweetheart belongs to David and Bonnie Prell.

dog ownership involves is one of the primary reasons there are so many unwanted canines forced to end their lives in an animal shelter.

Before anyone contemplates the purchase of a dog there are some very important conditions that must be considered. One of the first important questions that must be answered is whether or not the person who will ultimately be responsible for the dog's care and well being actually wants a dog.

If the prospective dog owner lives alone, all he or she needs do is be sure that there is a strong desire to make the necessary commitment dog ownership entails. In the case of family households, it is vital that the person who will ultimately be responsible for the dog's care really wants a dog. In the average household, mothers, even working mothers, are most often given the additional responsibility of caring for the family pets. Irrespective of the fact that nowadays mothers too are out in the workplace, all too often they are saddled with the additional chores of feeding and trips to the veterinary hospital with what was supposed to be the family pet.

Pets are a wonderful method of teaching children responsibility but it should be remembered that the enthusiasm that inspires children to promise anything in order to have a new puppy may quickly wane. Who will take care of the puppy once the novelty wears off? Does that person want a dog?

Desire to own a dog aside, does the lifestyle of the family actually provide for responsible dog ownership? If the entire family is away from home from early morning to late at night, who will provide for all of a puppy's needs? Feeding, exercise, outdoor access and the like can not be provided if no one is home.

Another important factor to consider is whether or not the breed of dog is suitable for the person or the family with which it will be living. Some breeds can handle the rough and tumble play of young children. Some cannot. On the other hand, some dogs are so large and clumsy, especially as puppies, that they could easily and unintentionally injure an infant.

Then too, there is the matter of hair. A luxuriously coated dog is certainly beautiful to behold but all that hair takes care. In the case of a Samoyed a quick pass over with a brush when the mood strikes will not suffice. Brushing an adult Samoyed requires time and elbow grease. Both long-and short-haired dogs shed their coats in the home. Naturally the longer hair of

A purebred puppy will grow to closely resemble his adult relatives. This Sammy pup snuggles close to his dad.

the Sammy is more noticeable and if not kept after, will deposit itself in every nook and cranny of the household.

As great as claims are for any breed's intelligence and trainability, remember the new dog must be taught every household rule that it is to observe. Some dogs catch on more quickly than others and puppies are just as inclined to forget or disregard lessons as young children are.

In terms of grooming, the Samoyed is a high-maintenance dog. The time you want to spend on grooming should be a consideration before choosing a breed.

CASE FOR THE PUREBRED DOG

As previously mentioned all puppies are cute. Not all puppies grow up to be particularly attractive adults. What is considered beauty by one person is not necessarily seen as attractive by another. It is almost impossible to

The Sammy makes a wonderful companion for children and enjoys all aspects of family life—including an afternoon nap!

determine what a mixed breed puppy will look like as an adult. Nor will it be possible to determine if the mixed breed puppy's temperament is suitable for the person or family who wishes to own it. If the puppy grows up to be too big, too hairy or too active for the owner, what then will happen to him?

Size and temperament can vary to a degree even within a purebred breed. Still, selective breeding over many generations has produced dogs giving the would-be owner reasonable assurance of what the purebred puppy will look and act like as an adult. Points of attractiveness completely aside, this predictability is more important than one might think.

A person who wants a dog to go along on those morning jogs or long distance runs is not going to be particularly happy with a lethargic or short-legged breed. Nor is the fastidious housekeeper, whose picture of the ideal dog is one that lies quietly at the feet of his master by the hour and never sheds, going to be particularly happy with the shaggy dog whose temperament is reminiscent of a hurricane.

Purebred puppies will grow up to look like their adult relatives and by and large they will behave pretty much like the rest of their family. Any dog, mixed breed or not, has the potential to be a loving companion. However, a purebred dog offers reasonable insurance that he will not only suit the owner's lifestyle but the person's esthetic demands as well.

WHO SHOULD OWN A SAMOYED?

Just as a prospective buyer should have a check list to lead him or her to a responsible breeder, so do good breeders have a list of qualifications for the buyer. These are just a few of the "musts" for a prospective Sammy owner:

1. The buyer must have a fenced yard.

2. The dog can not be made to live exclusively outdoors.

3. Young, single or unsettled people are poor candidates. The future spouse usually wants a different breed.

4. Children must be over four years of age except in very special cases.

5. Everyone in the family must want a Samoyed. Both the husband and wife must be interviewed to determine their desire to own a Sammy.

6. The buyer must be financially able to provide proper veterinary and home care.

7. No Samoyed to parties who are interested in mass producing Samoyeds or operating an indiscriminate "stud factory."

As sturdy a constitution as the Samoyed may have and as high as his tolerance for discomfort might be, a Sammy is completely incapable of withstanding being struck in anger. This devastates the Samoyed and if subjected to treatment of this nature on a continuing basis it can turn even the most amiable youngster into a neurotic and unpredictable adult.

This is not to say the Sammy owner needs to or should be passive in raising and training his or her dog. On the contrary, a young Samoyed must start understanding household rules from the first moment he comes into your home. What it will take to accomplish this is the aforementioned patience and a firm but gentle and unrelenting hand. Even the youngest Samoyed puppy understands the difference between being corrected and being abused.

A trio of strikingly beautiful Samoyeds in their natural element.

Someone who needs a dog that does well living outdoors with minimal owner interaction should in all fairness look to

another breed. The Samoyed must have constant human companionship and social interaction not only with his owner, but with all kinds of people and other dogs. This is essential to the well being of the Samoyed.

Needless-to-say, the Samoyed owner must be prepared to take care of the breed's coat. The heavier the coat and the larger the dog, the more time and effort will be required. This is particularly so when the Samoyed begins to shed. While tangles and matting are not a problem in the mature Samoyed with the proper coat, the shedding does continue on a semiannual basis. The responsible owner should allow an hour or so at least once a week for general coat and health care.

CHARACTER OF THE SAMOYED

The Samoyed is very people-oriented, intelligent, dignified, and generally very good with well-behaved children. The breed is active, hardy and has very few health problems. The well cared for Samoyed has no doggie odor, a long life span and adapts well to most environments whether it be living on a ranch or in an apartment. Just so long as a Samoyed can be with his family, he is happy to do his hiking around the block or up a mountain side.

While the Samoyed requires regular grooming and brushing, especially during seasonal "coat blowing," most Sammy owners consider the fact the breed has no doggie odor a fair trade-off. The coat is actually easier to keep up than most would think because of its resilient water-resistant and dirt-resistant double coat.

The Samoyed can make a good watch dog as he is a lively barker when excited, alerted or happy. As with any arctic breed, the Sammy is an independent thinker. The breed is extremely clean and makes

The well-trained Samoyed strives to please his master and eagerly waits for every command.

Never underestimate a Sammy pup's ability to get into a tight spot! This Samoyed pup takes a snooze in an unusual spot

a wonderful house dog. Housebreaking usually takes much less time than it does with many other breeds.

Samoyed puppies can be extremely mischievous, devout chewers and they, like most growing puppies, can be very destructive. Never put anything beyond the Samoyed puppy's ingenuity!

A special characteristic of the Samoyed is his ability to be trained to work and yet keep his amiable disposition. One seldom sees a Sammy become surly because of the demands put upon him by an owner. In fact the AKC standard states clearly under "disposition" that the breed be "...alert, full of action, eager to serve..." Sammies do serve well and in many capacities ranging from sled dog to herding dog, watch dog to obedience and therapy dogs. Their most cherished role, however, is that of companion to man.

STANDARD of the Samoyed

The standard of the Samoyed is written in a simple and straightforward manner that can be read and understood by even the beginning fancier. It takes many years of experience and observation, however, to fully grasp all of the standard's implications. Reading as much about the breed as possible helps a great deal, but there is nothing as beneficial as putting yourself in the hands of a dedicated and experienced breeder if you sincerely wish to develop your knowledge of the breed.

Author Terry Campbell is pictured handling Marchwood's Dutch Clover to one of the many wins that took her to her championship.

General Conformation:

***(a) General Appearance*—The** Samoyed, being essentially a working dog, should present a picture of beauty, alertness and strength, with agility, dignity and grace. As his work lies in cold climates, his coat should be heavy and weather-resistant, well groomed, and of good quality rather then quantity. The male carries more of a "ruff" than the female. He should not be long in the back as a weak back would make him practically useless for his legitimate work, but at the same time, a close-coupled body would also place him at a great disadvantage as a draft dog. Breeders should aim for the happy medium, a body not long but muscular, allowing liberty, with a deep chest and well-sprung ribs, strong neck, straight front and especially strong loins. Males should be masculine in appearance and deportment without unwarranted

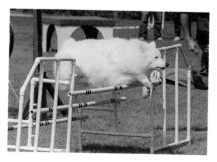

The Samoyed is a working dog whose appearance should reflect beauty, strength, agility and grace.

aggressiveness; bitches feminine without weakness of structure or apparent softness of temperament. Bitches may be slightly longer in back than males. They should both give the appearance of being *Author Gail Campbell is pictured with the top winning American Samoyed, Am. Int.Ch. Tega's Joe Knows, TT.*
capable of great endurance but be free from coarseness. Because of the depth of chest required, the legs should be moderately long. A very short-legged dog is to be deprecated. Hindquarters should be particularly well developed, stifles well bent and any suggestion of unsound stifles or cowhocks severely penalized. General appearance should include movement and general conformation, indicating balance and good substance.

(b) Substance—Substance is that sufficiency of bone and muscle which rounds out a balance with the frame. The bone

is heavier than would be expected in a dog of this size but not so massive as to prevent the speed and agility most desirable in a Samoyed. In all builds, bone should be in proportion to body size. The Samoyed should never be so heavy as to appear clumsy nor so light as to appear racy. The weight should be in proportion to the height.

(c) Height—Males—21 to 23 ½ inches; females—19 to 21 inches at the withers. An oversized or undersized Samoyed is to be penalized according to the extent of the deviation.

(d) Coat (Texture & Condition)—The Samoyed is a doublecoated dog. The body should be well covered with an undercoat of soft, short, thick, close wool with longer and harsh hair growing through it to form the outer coat, which stands straight out from the body and should be free from curl. The coat should form a ruff around the neck and shoulders, framing the head (more on males than on females). Quality of coat should be weather resistant and considered more than quantity. A droopy coat is undesirable. The coat should glisten with a silver sheen. The female does not usually carry as long a coat as most males and it is softer in texture.

The Samoyed should move freely, with a balanced and vigorous stride.

(e) Color—Samoyeds should be pure white, white and biscuit, cream, or all biscuit. Any other colors disqualify.

Movement:

(a) Gait—The Samoyed should trot, not pace. He should move with a quick agile stride that is well timed. The gait should be free, balanced and vigorous, with good reach in the forequarters and good driving power in the hindquarters. When trotting, there should be a strong rear action drive. Moving at a slow walk or trot, they will not single-track, but as speed increases the legs gradually angle inward until the pads are finally falling on a line directly under the longitudinal center of the body. As the pad marks converge the forelegs and

hind legs are carried straight forward in traveling, the stifles not turned in nor out. The back should remain strong, firm and level. A choppy or stilted gait should be penalized.

(b) Rear End—Upper thighs should be well developed. Stifles well bent—approximately 45 degrees to the ground. Hocks should be well developed, sharply defined and set at approximately 30 percent of hip height. The hind legs should be parallel when viewed from the rear in a natural stance, strong, well developed, turning neither in nor out. Straight stifles are objectionable. Double-jointedness or cowhocks are a fault. Cowhocks should only be determined if the dog has had an opportunity to move properly.

Int. Am. Ch. Tega's Joe Knows, TT is an outstanding representative of all the qualities called for in the Samoyed breed standard.

(c) Front End—Legs should be parallel and straight to the pasterns. The pasterns should be strong, sturdy and straight, but flexible with some spring for proper let-down of feet. Because of depth of chest, legs should be moderately long. Length of leg from the ground to the elbow should be approximately 55 per cent of the total height at the withers—a very short-legged dog is to be deprecated. Shoulders should be long and sloping, with a layback of 45 degrees and be firmly set. Out at the shoulders or out at the elbows should be penalized. The withers separation should be approximately 1-1 $^1/_2$ inches.

(d) Feet—Large, long, flattish-a hare-foot, slightly spread but not splayed; toes arched; pads thick and tough, with protective growth of hair between the toes. Feet should turn neither in nor out in a natural stance but may turn in slightly in the act of pulling. Turning out, pigeon-toed, round or cat-footed or splayed are faults. Feathers on feet are not too essential but are more profuse on females than on males.

A Samoyed's ears should be strong, thick, erect and triangular in shape.

Head:

(a) Conformation—Skull is wedge-shaped, broad, slightly crowned, not round or apple-headed, and should form an equilateral triangle on lines between the inner base of the ears and the central point of the stop. **Muzzle**—Muzzle of medium length and medium width, neither coarse nor snipy; should taper toward the nose and be in proportion to the size of the dog and the width of skull. The muzzle must have depth. Whiskers are not to be removed. **Stop**—Not too abrupt, nevertheless well defined. **Lips**—Should be black for preference and slightly curved up at the corners of the mouth, giving the "Samoyed smile." Lip lines should not have the appearance of being coarse nor should the flews drop predominately at corners of the mouth.

Ears—Strong and thick, erect, triangular and slightly rounded at the tips; should not be large or pointed, nor should they be small and "bear-eared." Ears should conform to head size and the size of the dog; they should be set well apart but be within the border of the outer edge of the head; they should be mobile and well covered inside with hair; hair full and stand-off before the ears. Length of ear should be the same measurement as the distance from inner base of ear to outer corner of eye.

Eyes—Should be dark for preference; should be placed well apart and deep-set; almond shaped with lower lid slanting toward an imaginary point approximately the base of ears. Dark eye rims for preference. Round or protruding eyes penalized. Blue eyes disqualifying.

Nose—Black for preference but brown, liver, or Dudley nose not penalized. Color of nose sometimes changes with age and weather.

Jaws and Teeth—Strong, well-set teeth, snugly overlapping with scissors bite. Undershot or overshot should be penalized.

(b) Expression—The expression, referred to as "Samoyed expression," is very important and is indicated by sparkle of the eyes, animation and lighting up of the face when alert or intent on anything. Expression is made up of a combination of eyes, ears and mouth. The ears should be erect when alert; the mouth should be slightly curved up at the corners to form the "Samoyed smile."

Torso:

(a) Neck—Strong, well muscled, carried proudly erect, set on sloping shoulders to carry head with dignity when at attention. Neck should blend into shoulders with a graceful arch.

(b) Chest—Should be deep, with ribs well sprung out from the spine and flattened at the sides to allow proper movement of the shoulders and freedom for the front legs. Should not be barrel-chested. Perfect depth of chest approximates the point of elbows, and the deepest part of the chest should be back of the forelegs-near the ninth rib. Heart and lung room are secured more by body depth than width.

(c) Loin and Back—The withers forms the highest part of the back. Loins strong and slightly arched. The back should be straight to the loin, medium in length, very muscular and neither long nor short-coupled. The dog should be "just off square"—the length being approximately 5 per cent more than the height. Females allowed to be slightly longer than males.

The belly should be well shaped and tightly muscled and, with the rear of the thorax, should swing up in a pleasing curve (tuck-up). Croup must be full, slightly sloping, and must continue imperceptibly to the tail root.

Tail—The tail should be moderately long with the tail bone terminating approximately at the hock when down. It should be profusely covered with long hair and carried forward over the back or side when alert, but sometimes dropped when at rest. It should not be high or low set and should be mobile and loose-not tight over the back. A double hook is a fault. A judge should see the tail over the back once when judging.

Disposition—Intelligent, gentle, loyal, adaptable, alert, full of action, eager to serve, friendly but conservative, not distrustful or shy, not overly aggressive. Unprovoked aggressiveness is to be severely penalized.

The Samoyed is an alert intelligent dog who is eager to please his master.

DISQUALIFICATIONS

Any color other than pure white, cream, biscuit, or white and biscuit.

Blue eyes.

Approved August 10, 1993
Effective September 29, 1993

SELECTING the Right Samoyed for You

O nce the prospective Samoyed owner satisfactorily answers all the questions relating to responsible ownership, he or she will undoubtedly want to rush out and purchase a puppy immediately. Take care—do not act in haste. The purchase of any dog is an important step since the well cared for dog will live with you for many years. In the case of a Samoyed this could easily be 12, 14 or perhaps even 15 years. You will undoubtedly want the dog you live with for that length of time to be one you will enjoy.

It is extremely important in this breed, as it is in any large breed of dog, that your Samoyed is purchased from a breeder who has earned a reputation over the years for consistently producing dogs that are mentally and physically sound. There are always those who are ready and willing to exploit a breed for financial gain with no thought given to his health or welfare, or to the homes in which the dogs will be living.

The only way a breeder can earn a reputation for quality is through a well thought out breeding program in which rigid selectivity is imposed. Selective breeding is aimed at maintaining the virtues of a breed and eliminating genetic weaknesses. This process is time consuming and costly.

Although they are of Russian heritage, these three little guys are true all-Americans!

Therefore, responsible Samoyed breeders protect their investment by providing the utmost in prenatal care for their brood matrons and maximum care and nutrition for the resulting offspring. Once the puppies arrive, the knowledgeable breeder initiates a well thought out socialization process.

Once separated from his mother and littermates, your Samoyed puppy will depend on his new owner to take care of all his needs.

The buyer should look for cleanliness in both the dogs and the areas in which the dogs are kept. Cleanliness is the first clue that tells you how much the breeder cares about the dogs he or she owns.

The governing kennel clubs in the different countries of the world maintain lists of local breed clubs and breeders that can lead a prospective dog buyer to responsible breeders of quality stock. Should you not be sure of where to contact a respected breeder in your area, we strongly recommend contacting your local kennel club for recommendations.

There is every possibility that a reputable breeder resides in your area who will not only be able to provide the right Sammy for you, but who will often have both parents of the puppy on the premises as well. This gives you an opportunity to see first hand what kind of dogs are in the background of the puppy you are considering. Good breeders are not only willing to have you see their dogs but to inspect the facility where the dogs are raised as well. These breeders will also be able to discuss problems that exist in the breed with you and how they deal with these problems.

The number one rule in determining what kind of a breeder you are speaking to is to ask what else they do with their Sammies besides simply keeping and breeding them. This will give you a good clue to their level of commitment to the breed. If they are just breeding Sammies to raise and sell puppies—look elsewhere! Find out if they show their dogs and if they work their dogs. A good part of the wonderful character of the Samoyed is his great versatility. A responsible breeder does everything possible to provide his dogs with every avenue possible to enhance this ability.

As we have mentioned previously, do not be surprised if a concerned breeder asks many questions about you and the environment in which your Sammy will be raised. Good breeders are just as concerned with the quality of the homes to which their dogs are going as you, the buyer are in obtaining a sound and healthy dog.

Do not think a good Samoyed puppy can only come from a large kennel. On the contrary, today many of the best breeders raise dogs in their homes as a hobby. It is important, however, that you not allow yourself to fall into the hands of an irresponsible "backyard breeder." Backyard breeders separate themselves from the hobby breeder through their lack of responsibility to use their stock to its full potential. A hobby breeder's

It's hard to believe that this little white puppy will grow up to be the majestic Samoyed. Barron's Appassionata Sonata and puppy.

dogs find their way into the show and obedience ring or participating in the many and varied pursuits in which the breed excels.

HEALTH CONCERNS

All breeds of dogs have genetic problems that must be paid attention to and just because a male and female do not show problems, this does not mean their pedigrees are free of something that might be entirely incapacitating. Again, rely upon recommendations from national kennel clubs or local breed clubs when looking for a breeder.

Pretty as a picture! The Sammy pup you choose should have bright eyes and radiate good health.

Like many other breeds, the Samoyed is subject to hip dysplasia—a deformity of the hip joints. Therefore responsible breeders work with test-bred stock and are very much aware of where it does and does not exist.

Susceptibility to allergies is an inherited trait. A Samoyed that is constantly suffering from skin eruptions and irritations or one that comes from a line prone to such problems is certainly not a good choice as a companion nor is it one that should ever be bred from.

Again, it is important that both the buyer and the seller ask questions. We would be highly suspect of a person who is willing to sell you a Samoyed with "no questions asked."

RECOGNIZING A HEALTHY PUPPY

Most breeders do not release their puppies until the puppies have been given their "puppy shots." Normally, this is at about seven to nine weeks of age. At this age they will bond extremely well with their new owners and the puppies are entirely weaned. Beware of a litter that is still together past 12 weeks of age. There could be socialization problems down the road. Puppies by this age have bonded to each other rather to a human being. Again, seven to nine weeks of age is absolutely an ideal age to select your Sammy puppy.

Nursing puppies receive temporary immunization from their mother. Once weaned, however, a puppy is highly susceptible to many infectious diseases that can be transmitted via the

Sammy puppies are irresistible, but make sure the decision to take one home is a carefully considered one. hands and clothing of people. Therefore, it behooves you to make sure your puppy is fully inoculated before it leaves its home environment and to know when any additional inoculations should be given.

Above all, the Sammy puppy you buy should be a happy, bouncy extrovert. The worst thing you could possibly do is buy a shy, shrinking-violet puppy or one that appears sick and listless because you feel sorry for it. Doing this will undoubtedly lead to heartache and difficulty to say nothing of the veterinary costs that you may incur in getting the puppy well.

If at all possible, take the puppy you are interested in away from his littermates into another room or another part of the kennel. The smells will remain the same for the puppy so he should still feel secure and maintain his outgoing personality, but it will give you an opportunity to inspect the puppy more closely. A healthy little Sammy puppy will be strong and sturdy to the touch, never bony, or on the other hand obese and bloated. The inside of the puppy's ears should be pink and clean. Dark discharge or a bad odor could indicate ear mites, a sure sign of poor maintenance. The healthy Sammy puppy's breath smells sweet. The teeth are clean and white and there should never be any malformation of the mouth or jaw. The puppy's eyes should be clear, bright and have that little twinkle so typical of a Sammy baby. Eyes that appear runny and irritated indicate serious problems.

It is important that a Samoyed puppy has time to socialize with his littermates in order to learn how to interact with other dogs.

There should be no sign of discharge from the nose nor should it be crusted or runny. Coughing or diarrhea are danger signals as are any eruptions on the skin. The coat should be soft and lustrous.

The healthy Sammy puppy's front legs should be straight as little posts and the movement light and bouncy. The best way to describe a Sammy puppy's movement is like that of a mechanical windup toy with legs that cover considerable ground. Of course there is always a chubby, clumsy puppy or two in a litter. Do not mistake this for unsoundness but if ever you have any doubts, discuss them with the breeder.

MALE OR FEMALE?

While both the male and the female are capable of becoming excellent companions and are equally easy to housebreak, do consider the fact that a male Sammy will mature considerably larger than his female littermates. He will weigh considerably more and in most cases have a good deal more coat. These are factors that should be taken into consideration as they require greater maintenance time on the part of the owner.

There are other sex related differences to consider as well. While the Samoyed is a clean breed and relatively easy to housebreak, the male provides a problem in that respect that is sexually related. The male of any breed of dog has a natural instinct to lift his leg and "mark" his territory. The amount of effort that is involved in training the male not to do this varies with the individual dog. What must be remembered is that a male considers everything in the household a part of his territory and has an innate urge to establish the fact. This unfortunately may include your designer drapery or newly upholstered sofa.

Females on the other hand have their own set of problems. Females have their semiannual heat cycles once they have passed one year of age. During these heat cycles of approximately 21 days the female must be confined to avoid soiling her surroundings with the bloody discharge that accompanies estrus. She must also be carefully watched to prevent males from gaining access to her or she will become pregnant.

Both of these sexually related problems can be avoided by having the pet Samoyed "altered." Spaying the female and neutering the male saves the pet owner all the headaches of either of the sexually related problems without changing the character of the Sammy. If there is any change at all in the altered Samoyed it is in making the dog an even more amiable companion. Above all, altering your pet precludes the possibility of him adding to the serious pet overpopulation problem that exists worldwide.

SELECTING A SHOW PROSPECT PUPPY

Should you be considering a show career for your puppy all the foregoing regarding soundness and health apply here as well. It must be remembered though, spaying and castration are not reversible procedures and once done they eliminate the possibility of ever breeding or showing your Samoyed in conformation shows. Altered dogs can, however, be shown in Obedience Trials.

There are a good number of additional points to be

considered for the show dog as well. First of all, it should be remembered that the most any breeder can offer is an opinion on the "show potential" of a particular puppy. The most promising eight-week-old puppy can grow up to be a mediocre adult. A breeder has no control over this.

Any predictions breeders make about a puppy's future are based upon their experience with past litters that have produced winning show dogs. It is obvious that the more successful a breeder has been in producing winning Samoyeds over the years, the broader his or her base of comparison will be.

A puppy's potential as a show dog is determined by how closely he adheres to the demands of the standard of the breed. While most breeders concur there is no such thing as "a sure thing" when it comes to predicting winners, they are also quick to agree that the older a puppy is, the better are your chances of making any predictions. We have found grading a litter and evaluating the puppies is best done at eight weeks of age.

If you must leave your puppy home alone, make sure he is in a safe enclosure with plenty of water, food and toys to keep him occupied.

It makes little difference to the owner of a pet if his Samoyed is a bit too small or if an ear hangs down a bit. Neither would it make a difference if a male pup had only one testicle. These faults do not interfere with a Samoyed becoming a healthy, loving companion. However, these flaws would keep that Samoyed from a winning show career.

While it certainly behooves the prospective buyer of a show prospect puppy to be as familiar with the standard of the breed as possible, it is even more important for the buyer to put his or her self into the hands of a successful and respected breeder of winning Sammies. The experienced breeder knows there are certain age-related shortcomings in a young Samoyed that maturity will take care of and other faults which completely eliminate it from consideration as a show prospect. Also, breeders are always looking for the right homes in which to place their show prospect puppies and will be particularly helpful when they know you plan to show one of their dogs.

Dogs will be dogs! Staying true to his ancestry, this Samoyed puppy howls at the moon.

The important thing to remember in choosing your first show prospect is that "cuteness" may not be consistent with quality. An extroverted puppy in the litter might decide he belongs to you. If you are simply looking for a pet, that is the Samoyed puppy for you. However, if you are genuinely interested in showing your Samoyed, you must keep your head. Without disregarding good temperament, give serious consideration to what the standard says a show type Sammy must be.

Look for the pup in a litter that is sound—both mentally and physically. He must have an outgoing and confident attitude. A Samoyed without a feeling of self importance will seldom develop into an outstanding show dog.

Any puppy that appears short on its legs or too long in his body should not be considered at all for the show ring. The overall impression is of a little tank—broad and sturdy from one end to the other.

You want a puppy with strong, straight, gun-barrel front legs. A spindly looking pup is all wrong for a Samoyed. The tail should be carried up and curved over the back.

There are many nuances of breed type that are best understood by an experienced breeder of show quality

Samoyeds. Rely upon someone who has had this experience to assist you in selecting a puppy of promise. There is an

Even if your Samoyed possesses physical faults, he still can be a wonderful pet.

old breeder's saying that applies well here. "Breed the best to the best. Select the best and then hope for the best!"

PUPPY OR ADULT?

A young puppy is not your only option when contemplating the purchase of a Samoyed. In some cases an adult dog may be just the answer. It certainly eliminates the trials and tribulations of housebreaking, chewing and the myriad of other problems associated with a young puppy.

On occasion, adult Sammies are available from kennels or homes breeding show dogs. Their breeders realize that an older Sammy would be far happier in a family situation where he can watch TV, take hikes and be a part of a family instead of living out his life in a kennel run.

Adult Sammies seem to adjust to their new homes with great enthusiasm. Most new owners are amazed at how quickly it all happens and how quickly these adults become devoted to their new families!

Your Samoyed breeder will have started socializing your puppy with different people and situations. These puppies explore the yard for the first time.

An adult Sammy that comes from a kind and loving environment could be the perfect answer for an elderly person or someone who is forced to be away from home during the day. While it would be unreasonable to expect a young puppy not to relieve himself in the house if you are gone for more than just a few hours, it would be surprising to find a housebroken Sammy who in adulthood would willingly even consider relieving himself in the home in which he lives.

A few adult Sammies may have become set in their ways and while you may not have to contend with the problems of puppyhood, do realize there is the rare adult that might have developed habits which do not entirely suit you or your lifestyle. Arrange to bring an adult Sammy into your home on a trial basis. That way neither you nor the dog will be obligated

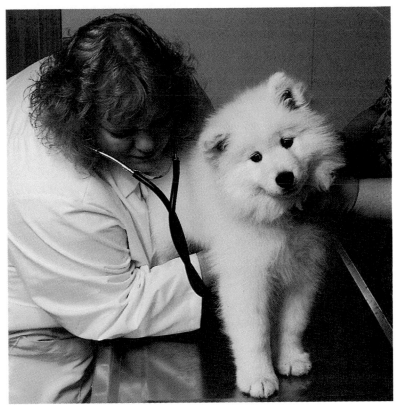

You should take your new Sammy pup to the veterinarian within 48 hours of taking him home.

should either of you decide you are incompatible.

IDENTIFICATION PAPERS

The purchase of any purebred dog entitles you to four very important documents: a health record containing an inoculation list, a copy of the dog's pedigree, the dog's registration certificate and the diet sheet.

Health Record

Most Sammy breeders have initiated the necessary inoculation series for their puppies by the time they are eight weeks of age. These inoculations protect the puppies against hepatitis, leptospirosis, distemper and canine parvovirus. In most cases, rabies inoculations are not given until a puppy is six months of age or older.

There is a set series of inoculations developed to combat these infectious diseases and it is extremely important that you obtain a record of the shots your puppy has been given and the dates that the shots were administered. This way, the veterinarian you choose will be able to continue on with the appropriate inoculation series as needed.

Pedigree

The pedigree is your dog's "family tree." The breeder must supply you with a copy of this document authenticating your puppy's ancestors back to at least the third generation. All purebred dogs have a pedigree. The pedigree does not imply that a dog is of show quality. It is simply is a chronological list of ancestors.

Registration Certificate

The registration certificate is the canine world's "birth certificate." This certificate is issued by a country's governing kennel club. When you transfer the ownership of your Sammy from the breeder's name to your own name, the transaction is entered on this certificate. Once it is mailed to the club, it is permanently recorded in their computerized files. Keep all these documents in a safe place, as you will need them when you visit your veterinarian or should you ever wish to breed or show your Sammy.

Diet Sheet

Your Samoyed is the happy healthy puppy it is because the breeder has been carefully feeding and caring for it. Every

Your breeder will have started your pup on the road to good nutrition, so stick to this original diet.

breeder we know has his own particular way of doing this. Most breeders give the new owner a written record that details the amount and kind of food a puppy has been receiving. Follow these recommendations to the letter at least for the first month or two after the puppy comes to live with you.

The diet sheet should indicate the number of times a day your puppy has been accustomed to being fed and the kind of vitamin supplementation, if any, he has been receiving. Following the prescribed procedure will reduce the chance of upset stomach and loose stools.

Look at the puppy you are considering away from his littermates. He should be playful, healthy-looking and curious about the world around him.

Usually a breeder's diet sheet projects the increases and changes in food that will be necessary as your puppy grows from week to week. If the sheet does not include this information ask the breeder for suggestions regarding increases and the eventual changeover to adult food.

In the unlikely event you are not supplied with a diet sheet by the breeder and are unable to get one, your veterinarian will be able to advise you in this respect. There are countless foods now being manufactured expressly to meet the nutritional needs of puppies and growing dogs. A trip down the pet aisle at your supermarket or pet supply store will prove just how many choices you have. Read labels carefully for content, and deal with established, reliable manufacturers—you are more likely to get what you pay for.

HEALTH GUARANTEE

Any reputable breeder is more than willing to supply a written agreement that the sale of your Sammy is contingent upon his passing a veterinarian's examination. Ideally you will be able to arrange an appointment with your chosen veterinarian right after you have picked up your puppy from the breeder and before you take the puppy home. If this is not possible, you should not delay this procedure any longer than

24 hours from the time you take your puppy home.

TEMPERAMENT AND SOCIALIZATION

Temperament is both inherited and learned. Inherited good temperament can be ruined by poor treatment and lack of proper socialization. A Samoyed puppy that has inherited a bad temperament is a poor risk as either a companion or show dog and should certainly never be bred. Therefore, it is critical that you obtain a happy puppy from a breeder who is determined to produce good temperaments and has taken all the necessary steps to provide the early socialization necessary.

Temperaments in the same litter can range from strong willed and outgoing on the high end of the scale to reserved and retiring at the low end. A puppy that is so bold and strong-willed as to be foolhardy and uncontrollable could easily be a difficult adult that needs a very firm hand. This is hardly a dog for the owner who is mild and reserved in demeanor or frail in physique. In every human-canine relationship there must be a pack leader and a follower. In order to achieve his full potential the Samoyed must have an owner who remains in charge at all times.

It is important to remember a Sammy puppy may be as happy as a clam living at home with you and your family, but if the socialization begun by the breeder is not continued, that sunny disposition will not extend outside your front door. From the day the young Sammy arrives at your home, you must be committed to accompanying him upon an unending pilgrimage to meet and like all human beings and animals.

If you are fortunate enough to have children well past the toddler stage in the household or living nearby, your socialization task will be assisted considerably. Samoyeds raised with children seem to have a distinct advantage in socialization. The two seem to understand each other and in some way known only to the puppies and children themselves, they give each other the confidence to face the trying ordeal of growing up.

The children in your own household are not the only children your puppy should spend time with. It is a case of the more the merrier! Every child (and adult for that matter) that enters your household should be asked to pet your puppy.

Your puppy should go everywhere with you—the post

office, the market, to the shopping mall—wherever. Be prepared to create a stir wherever you go because the very reason that attracted you to the first Samoyed you met applies here as well. Everyone will want to pet your little "teddy bear" and there is nothing in the world better for him.

Should your puppy back off from a stranger, give the person a treat to offer your puppy. You must insist your young Sammy be amenable to the attention of all strangers—young and old, short and tall, and of all races. It is not up to your puppy to decide who it will or will not be friendly with. You are in charge. You must call the shots.

If your Samoyed has a show career in his future, there are other things in addition to just being handled that will have to be taught. All Samoyed show dogs must learn to have their mouths opened and inspected by the judge. The judge must be able to check the teeth. Males must be accustomed to having their testicles touched as the dog show judge must determine that all male dogs are "complete," which means there are two

It is up to you, the owner, to continue socializing your Samoyed puppy in order for him to achieve his potential as a companion and pet.

normal-sized testicles in the scrotum. These inspections must begin in puppyhood and be done on a regular and continuing basis.

All Samoyeds must learn to get on with other dogs as well as with humans. If you are fortunate enough to have a "puppy preschool" or dog training class nearby, attend with as much regularity as you possibly can. A young Sammy that has been exposed regularly to other dogs from puppyhood will learn to adapt and accept other dogs and other breeds much more readily than a Samoyed that seldom sees strange dogs.

THE ADOLESCENT SAMOYED

You will find it amazing how quickly the little ball of fur you first brought home begins to develop into a full-grown Samoyed. Some lines shoot up to full size very rapidly, others mature more slowly. A few Sammies pass through adolescence quite gracefully but at about nine months most become lanky and ungainly growing in and out of proportion seemingly from one day to the next.

Although a Samoyed makes a wonderful present, the holidays are the worst time to bring a puppy into a new home.

Somewhere between 12 to 18 months, your Samoyed will have attained his full height. However, body and coat development continue on

A Sammy loves his owner and doesn't care who knows it!

until two years of age in some lines and up to three or four in others.

Food needs increase during this growth period and the average Samoyed seems as if he can never get enough to eat. All Samoyeds pass through a period when the puppy coat is shed and the adult coat is beginning to come in. It is essential you give grooming all the attention it requires at this time to remove the dead puppy hair so the new coat can come through easily.

This adolescent period is a particularly important one. It is the time your Samoyed must learn all the household and social rules by which he will live for the rest of his life. Your patience and commitment during this time will not only produce a respected canine good citizen but will forge a bond between the two of you that will grow and ripen into a wonderful relationship.

CARING for Your Samoyed

FEEDING AND NUTRITION

The best way to make sure your Sammy puppy is obtaining the right amount and the correct type of food for his age is to follow the diet sheet provided by the breeder from whom you obtained your puppy. Do your best not to change the puppy's diet and you will be less apt to run into digestive problems and diarrhea. Diarrhea is very serious in young puppies. Puppies with diarrhea can dehydrate very rapidly causing severe problems and even death.

If it is necessary to change your puppy's diet for any reason, it should never be done abruptly. Begin by adding a tablespoon or two of the new food, gradually increasing the amount until the meal consists entirely of the new product.

The amount of food you give your Samoyed puppy should be adjusted carefully. Remember the healthy Sammy will eat just about anything and will quickly learn to pester you with those "I'm starved!" eyes. Do not give in. Do not "free-feed." Monitor your dog's daily food intake and weight. Do not be fooled by fur! Many Sammies become overweight and this leads to numerous health problems and shortened lives.

A rule of thumb is this: you should be able to feel the ribs and backbone with just a slight layer of fat and muscle over

Be sure to provide your Sammy pup with a well-balanced diet formulated especially for growth.

them. Reach into the fur regularly to see how your dog is doing and weigh him regularly. Mature males should average 55-70 pounds and females in the area of 35-50 pounds depending on size of dog and substance of bone.

It is important to remember that once the dog gets fat he will not exercise and will be even more prone to weight gain. A vicious cycle begins.

At eight weeks of age your Sammy puppy will be

If you stick to a consistent feeding schedule your Samoyed will always know when it is feeding time.

Puppies receive their first nutrition while nursing, but once your Sammy comes to his new home, it is up to you to provide him with a healthy diet.

eating three meals a day. By the time he is six months old the puppy can do well on two meals a day. If your dog does not eat the food offered, he is either not

hungry or not well. Your dog will eat when he is hungry. If you suspect the dog is not well, a trip to the veterinarian is in order.

By the time your Sammy puppy is 12 months old you can reduce feedings to one a day. This meal can be given either in the morning or evening. It is really a matter of choice on your part. There are two important things to remember: feed the main meal at the same time every day and make sure what you feed is nutritionally complete.

If you wish, the single meal can be cut in half and fed twice a day. A morning or night time snack of hard dog biscuits made especially for large dogs can also be given. These biscuits not only become highly anticipated treats by your Sammy but are genuinely helpful in maintaining healthy gums and teeth.

"Balanced" Diets

In order for a canine diet to qualify as "complete and balanced" in the United States, it must meet standards set by the Subcommittee on Canine Nutrition of the National Research Council of the National Academy of Sciences. Most commercial foods manufactured for dogs meet these standards and prove this by listing the ingredients contained in the food on every package and can. The ingredients are listed in descending order with the main ingredient listed first.

Fed with any regularity at all, refined sugars can cause your Samoyed to become obese and will definitely create tooth decay. Candy stores do not exist in the wild and canine teeth are not genetically disposed to handling sugars. Do not feed your Samoyed sugar products and avoid products that contain sugar to any high degree.

Fresh water and a properly prepared, balanced diet containing the essential nutrients in correct proportions are all a healthy Samoyed needs to be offered. Dog foods come canned, dry, semi-moist, "scientifically fortified" and "all-natural." A visit to your local supermarket or pet store will reveal how vast an array you will be able to select from.

The important thing to remember is that all dogs, whether they are Samoyeds or Dachshunds, are carnivorous (meat eating) animals. While the vegetable content of your dog's diet should not be overlooked, a dog's physiology and anatomy are based upon carnivorous food acquisition. Animal protein and fats are absolutely essential to the well being of your Samoyed. Dry foods seldom contain the amount of fat that will keep the healthy Samoyed in top condition. A small amount of animal fat such as bacon drippings or beef trimmings can be beneficial when added to the Samoyed's diet particularly during winter weather.

This having been said, it should be realized that in the wild carnivores eat the entire beast they capture and kill. The carnivore's kills consist almost entirely of herbivores (plant eating) animals and invariably the carnivore begins its meal with the contents of the herbivore's stomach. This provides the carbohydrates, minerals and nutrients present in vegetables.

The amount of food you give your dog will depend on his stage of life and level of activity. Blithe Spirit UD, HT, OA clears the bar jump.

Through centuries of domestication we have made our dogs entirely dependent upon us for their well being.

Therefore we are entirely responsible for duplicating the food balance the wild dog finds in nature. The domesticated dog's diet must include protein, carbohydrates, fats, roughage and small amounts of essential minerals and vitamins.

Finding commercially prepared diets that contain all the necessary nutrients will not present a problem. It is important to understand though, that these commercially prepared foods do contain all the necessary nutrients. It is therefore unnecessary to add vitamin supplements to these diets in other than special circumstances prescribed by your veterinarian. These "special" periods in a Samoyed's life include the time of rapid growth the breed experiences in puppyhood, the female's pregnancy and the time during which she is nursing her puppies. This is not a case of "if a little is good, more is better." Over-supplementation and forced growth are now looked upon by some breeders as major contributors to many skeletal abnormalities found in the purebred dogs of the day.

Over-Supplementation

A great deal of controversy exists today regarding orthopedic problems such as hip, elbow and patella (knee) dysplasia that afflict Samoyeds and many other breeds. Some claim these problems and a wide variety of chronic skin conditions are entirely hereditary but many others feel they can be exacerbated by diet and overuse of mineral and vitamin supplements for puppies.

Backpacking is an event in which Samoyeds have a natural talent.

In giving vitamin supplementation one should never exceed the prescribed amount. Some breeders insist all recommended dosages be halved before including them in a dog's diet because of the highly fortified commercial foods being fed. Still other breeders feel no supplementation should be given at all, believing a balanced diet that includes plenty of milk products and a small amount of bone meal to provide calcium is all that is necessary and beneficial.

If the owner of a Samoyed normally eats healthy nutritious food, there is no reason why his dog can not be given table scraps. What could possibly be harmful in good nutritious food? Table scraps should be given only as part of the dog's meal and never from the table. A Samoyed that becomes accustomed to being hand fed from the table can become a real pest at meal time very quickly. Also, dinner guests may find the pleading stare of your Sammy less than appealing when dinner is being served.

Dogs do not care if food looks like a hot dog or wedge of cheese. Truly nutritious dog foods are seldom manufactured to look like food that appeals to humans. Dogs only care about how food smells and tastes. It is highly doubtful you will be eating your dog's food so do not waste your money on these "looks just like" products.

Along these lines, most of the moist foods or canned foods which have the look of "delicious red beef" look that way because they contain great amounts of preservatives, sugars and dyes. These additives are no better for your dog than they are for you.

Special Diets

There are now any number of commercially prepared diets for dogs with special dietary needs. The overweight, underweight or geriatric dog can have its nutritional needs met as can puppies and growing dogs. The calorie content of these foods is adjusted accordingly. With the correct amount of the right foods and the proper amount of exercise, your Samoyed should stay in top shape. Common sense must prevail. What works for humans works for dogs as well—increasing calories will increase weight; stepping up exercise and reducing calories will bring weight down.

Occasionally a young Samoyed going through the teething period will become a finicky eater. The concerned owner's first response is to tempt the dog by handfeeding special treats and foods that the problem eater seems to prefer. This practice only serves to compound the problem. Once your dog learns to play the waiting game, he will turn up his nose at anything other than his favorite food knowing full well what he wants to eat will eventually arrive. Give your Samoyed the proper food you want him to eat. The dog may well turn up his nose a day or two and refuse to eat anything. However, you can rest assured when your dog is really hungry he will eat.

Unlike humans, dogs have no suicidal tendencies. A healthy dog will not starve himself to death. He may not eat enough to keep himself in the shape we find ideal and attractive but he will definitely eat enough to maintain himself. If your Samoyed is not eating properly and appears to be too thin, it is probably best to consult your veterinarian.

BATHING AND GROOMING

It is important to remember that the Samoyed is a natural breed that requires no clipping or trimming outside of tidying up his feet or perhaps removing the whiskers. Regular thorough brushing, a few snips of the scissors and a bath when needed are an important part of keeping your Samoyed clean, healthy and a pleasant companion. Consistent brushing and a wash cloth will keep the Samoyed's coat surprisingly clean but there are occasions where a full bath will be necessary.

Puppy Coat

Undoubtedly the breeder from whom you purchased your

Sammy puppy will have begun to accustom him to grooming just as soon as there was enough hair to brush—as early as two to three weeks of age.

You must continue on with grooming sessions or begin them at once if for some reason they have not been started. You and your Samoyed will spend a significant amount of time involved with this activity over a lifetime, so it is imperative that you both learn to cooperate in the endeavor to make it an easy and pleasant experience.

The easiest way to groom a Samoyed is by placing him on a grooming table. A grooming table can be built or purchased at your local pet shop. Make sure the table is of a height at which you can work comfortably either sitting or standing. Adjustable-height grooming tables are available at most pet outlets.

Because of his double white coat, proper grooming is a necessity in your Samoyed's daily routine.

Although you will buy this when your puppy first arrives, anticipate your dog's full grown size in making

your purchase and select or build a table that will accommodate a fully grown Samoyed. We use a grooming table that has an "arm" and a "noose." The noose slips around the dog's neck when he is standing and keeps the dog from fidgeting about or deciding he has had enough grooming.

You will need to invest in two brushes: a "pin" brush which has long wire bristles set in rubber for the long hair, and a "slicker" brush with shorter, angled bristles that are best used on the shorter hair of the head and feet. You will also need a steel comb to remove any debris that collects in the longer furnishings. A comb that has teeth divided between fine and coarse is ideal. Consider the fact you will be using this equipment for many years and buy the best of these items that you can afford.

Any attempt to groom your puppy on the floor may result with you spending a good part of your time chasing him around the room. Sitting on the floor for long stretches of time is also not the most comfortable position in the world for the average adult.

Your Samoyed must be accustomed to grooming procedures if he is to compete in dog shows.

When brushing, go through the coat from the skin out. Do this all over the body and be specially careful to attend to the hard-to-reach areas between the legs and under the body. Mats can occur rapidly during the time when the Sammy is shedding his puppy coat.

Should you encounter a mat that does not brush out easily use your fingers and the steel comb to separate the hairs as much as possible. Do not cut or pull out the matted hair. Apply baby powder or one of the specially prepared grooming powders directly to the mat and brush completely from the skin out.

Nail Trimming

This is a good time to accustom your Sammy to having his nails trimmed and having his feet inspected. Your puppy may not particularly like this part of its toilette, but with patience and the passing of time he will eventually resign himself to the fact that these "manicures" are a part of life. Nail trimming must be done with care in that it is important not to cut into the "quick." The Samoyed's dark nails make it difficult to see the quick which grows close to the end of the nail and contains very sensitive nerve endings. If the nail is allowed to grow too long it will be impossible to cut it back to a proper length without cutting into the quick. This causes severe pain to the dog and can also result in a great deal of bleeding that can be very difficult to stop.

The nails of a Samoyed who spends most of his time indoors or on grass when outdoors can grow long very quickly. Do not allow the nails to become overgrown and then expect to cut them back easily. If your Samoyed is getting plenty of exercise on cement or rough hard pavement, however, the nails may keep sufficiently worn down. If you notice the nails have become too long they must then be carefully trimmed back. Should the quick be nipped in the trimming process, there are a number of blood clotting products available at pet shops that will almost immediately stem the flow of blood. It is wise to have one of these products on hand in case there is a nail trimming accident or the dog tears a nail on his own.

There are coarse metal files available at pet shops that can be used in place of the nail clippers. This is a more gradual method of taking the nail back and one is far less apt to injure the quick.

Grooming the Adult Samoyed

Fortunately you and your Sammy have spent the many months between

When bathing your Samoyed, make sure to use a shampoo specially formulated for dogs.

puppyhood and full maturity learning to assist each other through the grooming process. The two of you have survived the shedding of the puppy coat and the arrival of the longer and far more abundant adult hair. While the method of grooming remains the same, there is more and longer hair to deal with. A thorough grooming session at least once a week is mandatory.

Experience has taught us that dry bath powders dry out the Samoyed coat and can lead to breaking the guard hairs. Thorough brushing while misting very lightly with either distilled water or a mixture of distilled water and conditioner goes a long way toward keeping the Samoyed clean between wet baths. We also use either rinseless shampoo or "baby wipes " for quick cleanups. This process will remove almost any accumulated debris that has collected in the hair. Well-kept Samoyeds are literally odor-free and frequent bathing is unnecessary.

Although his white coat acts as camouflage in the snow, there is no disguising the attractiveness of the Samoyed.

The Wet Bath

We always recommend bathing at shedding time as it helps remove the old coat. Otherwise, following the foregoing coat care procedure will all but eliminate the need for bathing a Samoyed more than a few times during the year. However, more frequent bathing is perfectly fine as long as you use a top quality dog shampoo. Professional grooming every eight weeks or so can go a long way toward maintaining the Samoyed in top condition.

If you do use a professional groomer, you must tell the groomer that a Samoyed should never be trimmed! The double coat not only protects the Samoyed from the cold, but also shields the Samoyed's skin from the heat of direct sunlight. Please remind your groomer of this fact and insist the only trimming that is to be done is to neaten up the feet and the rear pasterns (hocks).

On the occasion your Samoyed requires a wet bath you will need to gather the necessary equipment ahead of time. A rubber mat should be placed at the bottom of the tub to avoid your dog slipping and thereby becoming frightened. A rubber spray hose is absolutely necessary to thoroughly wet the Samoyed's dense coat. The hose is also necessary to remove all shampoo residue.

A small cotton ball placed inside each ear will avoid water running down into the dog's ear canal. Be very careful when washing around the eyes as soaps and shampoos can be extremely irritating. A tiny dab of petroleum jelly or a drop of mineral oil in each eye will help prevent shampoo from irritating the eye.

In bathing, start behind the ears and work back. Use a wash cloth to soap and rinse around the head and face. Once you have shampooed your dog, you must rinse the coat thoroughly and when you feel quite certain all shampoo residue has been removed, rinse once more. Shampoo residue in the coat is sure to dry the hair and could cause skin irritation.

What better way for a person to spend an autumn day than backpacking with a treasured companion? Debbie Haynes and "Holly" enjoy the great outdoors.

The Samoyed that is given plenty of opportunities to exercise is a happier and healthier dog. Foxy demonstrates his natural athleticism on the teeter totter.

As soon as you have completed the bath use heavy towels to remove as much of the excess water as possible. Your Samoyed will assist you in the process by shaking a great deal of the water out of his coat on his own.

Brush drying the coat with the assistance of a hair dryer (human or special canine blower-type) will reduce drying time significantly and will give the coat a standoff bloom that is truly beautiful. When using a hair dryer of any kind always keep the setting on "medium." Anything warmer can dry the coat and in extreme cases actually burn the skin.

EXERCISE

The Samoyed that is given plenty of opportunity to exercise is a much happier and healthier dog. Remember the breed's heritage—the Samoyed was bred to work a full day, every day!

Needless to say, puppies should never be forced to exercise.

Normally, they are little dynamos of energy and keep themselves busy all day long interspersed with frequent naps. Puppies can do fine in a large fenced yard but an adult Sammy does love a long, brisk, on-leash walk. Of course, this can do nothing but benefit the Sammy's owner as well.

It goes without saying that a romp in the snow is sheer heaven to a Samoyed! A trip to the mountains or to the North country could provide a day of sheer bliss for your friend.

Mature Samoyeds are not only capable of but are delighted to be jogging companions. They can also be exercised using a bicycle attachment made specifically for dogs. It is important, however, to use good judgment in any exercise program. Begin slowly and increase the distance to be covered very gradually over an extended period of time. Use special precautions in hot weather. High temperatures and forced exercise are a dangerous combination.

As an exercise partner, the Samoyed has no equal. These two friends enjoy a brisk walk on the beach.

SOCIALIZATION

The Samoyed comes into the world as a very people-oriented individual and constant exposure to people of all kinds does nothing but enhance the breed's marvelous personality. The breed's outstanding virtue perhaps is its capacity for companionship and a quiet friendly manner in all surroundings.

It should be understood however, that a young Sammy that has never been exposed to strangers, traffic noises or boisterous children could become confused and frightened. It is important that a Sammy owner give his or her dog the opportunity to experience all of these situations gradually and with its trusted owner present for support.

Socialization with littermates is very important. These two seem to be getting along just fine!

HOUSEBREAKING and Training Your Samoyed

There is no breed of dog that can not be trained. Some breeds are more difficult to get the desired response from than others. This has more to do with the trainer and his or her training methods than it does the dog's inability to learn. With the proper approach any dog that is not mentally deficient can be taught to be a good canine citizen. Many dog owners do not understand how a dog learns, nor do they realize they can be breed specific in their approach to training.

Young Samoyed puppies have an amazing capacity to learn. This capacity is greater than most humans realize. It is important to remember though, these young puppies also forget with great speed unless they are reminded of what they have learned by continual reinforcement.

As puppies leave the nest they began their search for two things: a pack leader and the rules set down by that leader by which they can abide. Because puppies, especially Sammy puppies, are cuddly and cute, some owners fail miserably in supplying these very basic needs. Instead, the owner immediately begins to respond to the demands of the puppy and puppies can quickly learn to be very demanding.

For example, a Sammy puppy quickly learns he will be allowed into the house because he is whining. Instead he should learn that he can only enter the house when he is *not* whining. Instead of learning the only way he will be fed is to follow a set procedure (i.e., sitting or lying down on command) the poorly educated Sammy puppy learns that leaping about the kitchen

When training your Samoyed, remember to keep the lesson short at first and to always make it fun for both you and your dog.

66

Double your fun? Two Sammys are better than one! and creating a stir is what gets results. If the young puppy can not find his pack leader in an owner, the puppy assumes the role of pack leader. If there are no rules imposed, the puppy learns to make his own rules. Unfortunately the negligent owner continually reinforces the puppy's decisions by allowing him to govern the household.

The key to successful training lies in establishing the proper relationship between dog and owner. The owner or the owning family must be the pack leader and the individual or family must provide the rules by which the dog abides.

The Samoyed is easily trained to do almost any task. It is important to remember, however, that the breed does not comprehend violent treatment nor does the Sammy need it. Positive reinforcement is the key to successfully training a Sammy. Always show your dog the right thing to do and be consistent in having him behave that way.

HOUSEBREAKING

The method of housebreaking we recommend is avoidance of accidents happening. We take a puppy outdoors to relieve

himself after every meal, after very nap and after every 15 or 20 minutes of playtime. We carry the puppy outdoors to avoid the opportunity of an accident occurring on the way.

Housebreaking your Sammy becomes a much easier task with the use of a crate. Most breeders use the fiberglass-type crates approved by the airlines for shipping live animals. They are easy to clean and can be used for the entire life of the dog.

Some first-time dog owners may see the crate method of housebreaking as cruel. What they do not understand is that all dogs need a place of their own to retreat to and Sammies in particular take well to crate training because they have a strong den instinct. A puppy will soon look to his crate as his own private den.

If you take your Samoyed outside to the same spot every time to eliminate, he will always know what is expected of him.

Use of a crate reduces housetraining time down to an absolute minimum and avoids keeping a puppy under constant stress by incessantly correcting him for making mistakes in the house. The anti-crate advocates who consider it cruel to confine a puppy for any length of time do not seem to have a problem with constantly harassing and punishing the puppy because he has wet on the carpet and relieved himself behind the sofa.

Begin using the crate to feed your Sammy puppy in. Keep the door closed and latched while the puppy is eating. When the meal is finished, open the cage and carry the puppy outdoors to the spot where you want him to learn to eliminate. In the event you do not have outdoor access or will be away from home for long periods of time, begin housebreaking by placing newspapers in some out of the way corner that is easily accessible for the puppy. If you consistently take your puppy to the same spot you will reinforce the habit of going there for that purpose.

Crate training is the easiest way to housebreak your Samoyed because dogs do not like to soil where they eat and sleep.

It is important that you do not let the puppy loose after eating. Young puppies will eliminate almost immediately after eating or drinking. They will also be ready to relieve themselves when they first wake up and after playing. If you keep a watchful eye on your puppy you will quickly learn when this is about to take place. A puppy usually circles and sniffs the floor just before he relieves himself. Do not give your puppy an opportunity to learn that he can eliminate in the house! Your house training chores will be reduced considerably if you avoid bad habits beginning in the first place.

If you are not able to watch your puppy every minute, he should be in his cage or crate with the door securely latched. Each time you put your puppy in the crate give him a small treat of some kind. Throw the treat to the back of the cage and encourage the puppy to walk in on his own. When he does so praise him and perhaps hand him another piece of the treat through the wires of the cage.

Do understand that a Sammy puppy of eight to twelve weeks will not be able to contain himself for long periods of time. Puppies of that age must relieve themselves often, except at night. Your schedule must be adjusted accordingly. Also make sure your puppy has relieved himself at night before the last member of the family retires.

Your Samoyed will come to think of his crate as a cozy retreat and a place to rest and relax.

A baby gate will keep your Samoyed safe and out of mischief if you have to leave him home alone.

Your first priority in the morning is to get the puppy outdoors. Just how early this will take place will depend much more upon your puppy than upon you. If your Sammy is like most others there will be no doubt in your mind when he needs to be let out. You will also very quickly learn to tell the difference between the puppy's "emergency" signals and just unhappy grumbling. Do not test the young puppy's ability to contain himself. His vocal demand to be let out is confirmation that the housebreaking lesson is being learned.

Should you find it necessary to be away from home all day you will not be able to leave your puppy in a crate but on the other hand do not make the mistake of allowing him to roam the house or even a large room at will. Confine the puppy to a small room or partitioned off area and cover the floor with newspaper. Make this area large enough so that the puppy will not have to relieve himself next to his bed, food or water bowls. You will soon find the puppy will be inclined to use one particular spot to perform his bowel and bladder functions. When you are home you must take the puppy to this exact spot to eliminate at the appropriate time.

The Samoyed is an easily trained breed who is eager to please his master.

BASIC TRAINING

Training should never take place when you are irritated, distressed or preoccupied. Nor should you begin basic training in crowded or noisy places that will interfere with you or your dog's concentration. Once the commands are understood and learned you can begin testing your dog in public places, but at first the two of you should work in a place where you can concentrate fully upon each other.

The "No!" Command

There is no doubt that one of the most important commands your Sammy puppy will ever learn is the meaning of "no!" It is extremely important that your puppy learn this command as soon as possible. One important piece of advice in using this and all other commands—never give a command you are not prepared and able to enforce! The only way a puppy learns to obey commands is to realize that once issued, commands must be complied with. Learning the "no" command should start the first day of the puppy's arrival at your home.

Leash Training

It is never too early to accustom your Sammy puppy to his leash and collar. The leash and collar are your fail-safe way of keeping your dog under control. It may not be necessary for the puppy or adult Samoyed to wear his collar and identification tags within the confines of your home but no dog should ever leave home without a collar and without the leash held securely in your hand.

Your Samoyed must learn to walk on a leash, for his safety and for the safety of others.

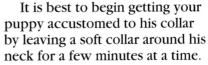

It is best to begin getting your puppy accustomed to his collar by leaving a soft collar around his neck for a few minutes at a time. Gradually extend the time you leave the collar on. Most Sammy puppies become accustomed to their collar very quickly and after a few scratches to remove it, forget they are even wearing one.

While you are playing with the puppy, attach a lightweight leash to the collar. Do not try to guide the puppy at first. The point here is to accustom the puppy to the feeling of having something attached to the collar.

Encourage your puppy to follow you as you move away. Should the puppy be reluctant to cooperate, coax him along with a treat of some kind. Hold the treat in front of the puppy's nose to encourage him to follow you. Just as soon as the puppy takes a few steps toward you, praise him enthusiastically and continue to do so as you continue to move along.

Make the initial sessions short and fun. Continue the lessons in your home or yard until the puppy is completely unconcerned about the fact that he is on a leash. With a treat in one hand and the leash in the other you can begin to use both to guide the puppy in the direction you wish to go. Begin your first walks in front of the house and eventually extend them down the street and around the block.

The "Come" Command

The next most important lesson for the Sammy puppy to learn is to come when called. Therefore is very important that the puppy learn his name as soon as possible. Constantly repeating the dog's name is what does the trick. Use the puppy's name every time you speak to him. "Want to go outside, Rex?" "Come Rex, come!"

Learning to "come" on command could save your Sammy's life when the two of you venture out into the world. "Come" is the command a dog must understand has to be obeyed without question, but the dog should not associate that command with fear. Your dog's response to his name and the word "come" should always be associated with a pleasant experience such as great praise and petting or a food treat.

All too often novice trainers get

Ch. Tarahill's Treasure Me Always, WSX, CGC, TDI owned by Joan Froling practices his recall exercises.

very angry at their dog for not responding immediately to the "come" command. When the dog finally does come or after a chase, the owner scolds the dog for not obeying. The dog begins to associate "come" with an unpleasant result.

It is much easier to avoid the establishment of bad habits than it is to correct them once set. Avoid at all costs giving the "come" command unless you are sure your Sammy puppy will come to you. The very young puppy is far more inclined to respond to learning the "come" command than the older dog. Use the command initially when the puppy is already on his way to you or give the command while walking or running away from the youngster. Clap your hands and sound very happy and excited about having the puppy join in on this "game."

Provide your Sammy pup with plenty of safe toys like Nylabones® to chew on.

The very young Sammy will normally want to stay as close to his owner as possible, especially in strange surroundings. When your puppy sees you moving away, his natural inclination will be to get close to you. This is a perfect time to use the "come" command.

Later, as a puppy grows more self confident and independent, you may want to attach a long leash or rope to his collar to insure the correct response. Again, do not chase or punish your puppy for not obeying the "come" command. Doing so in the initial stages of training makes the youngster associate the command with something to fear and this will result in avoidance rather than the immediate positive response you desire. It is imperative that you praise your puppy and give him a treat when he does come to you, even if he voluntarily delays responding for many minutes.

The "Sit" and "Stay" Commands

Just as important to your Sammy's safety (and your sanity!) as the "no" command and learning to come when called are the "sit" and "stay" commands. Even very young puppies can learn the sit command quickly, especially if it appears to be a game and a food treat is involved.

Your puppy should always be on collar and leash for his

lessons. Young puppies are not beyond getting up and walking away when he has decided you and your lessons are boring.

Give the "sit" command immediately before pushing down on your puppy's hindquarters or scooping his hind legs under the dog molding him into a sit position. Praise the puppy lavishly when he does sit, even though it is you who made the action take place. Again, a food treat always seems to get the lesson across to the learning youngster.

Continue holding the dog's rear end down and repeat the "sit" command several times. If your dog makes an attempt to get up, repeat the command yet again while exerting pressure on his rear end until the correct position is assumed. Make your Sammy stay in this position for increasing lengths of time. Begin with a few seconds and increase the time as lessons progress over the following weeks.

This group of Samoyeds from Ala-Kasam Kennels looks ready to go!

Should your young student attempt to get up or to lie down he should be corrected by simply saying, "sit!" in a firm voice. This should be accompanied by returning the dog to the desired position. Only when you decide your dog should get up should he be allowed to do so.

Do not test a very young puppy's patience to the limits. Remember you are dealing with a baby. The attention span of any youngster, canine or human, is relatively short.

When you do decide your puppy can get up, call his name, say "OK" and make a big fuss over it. Praise and a food treat are in order every time your puppy responds correctly.

Once your puppy has mastered the "sit" lesson you may start on the "stay" command. With your dog on leash and facing you, command him to "sit," then take a step or two back. If your dog attempts to get up to follow firmly say, "Sit, stay!" While you are saying this raise your hand, palm toward the dog, and again command "stay!"

A well-trained Samoyed is a joy to own. This Sammy demonstrates his sit.

Any attempt on your dog's part to get up must be corrected at once, returning him to the sit position and repeating, "stay!" Once your Sammy begins to understand what you want, you can gradually increase the distance you step back. With a long leash attached to your dog's collar (even a clothesline will do) start with a few steps and gradually increase the distance to several yards. Your Samoyed must eventually learn that the "Sit, stay" command must be obeyed no matter how far away you are. Later on, with advanced training, your dog will learn the command is to be obeyed even when you move entirely out of sight.

As your Sammy masters this lesson and is able to remain in the sit position for as long as you dictate, avoid calling the dog to you at first. This makes the dog overly anxious to get up and run to you. Instead, walk back to your dog and say "OK" which is a signal that the command is over. Later, when your Sammy becomes more reliable in this respect, you can call him to you.

The "sit, stay" lesson can take considerable time and patience especially with the Sammy puppy. It is best to keep the "stay" part of the lesson to a minimum until the puppy is at least five or six months old.

Samoyeds can be trained to participate in many events. These two Sammys owned by Barbara Cole are hooked up to a regulation wheeled rig used for carting.

Home is where the heart is and a Samoyed's heart belongs to his family.

Everything in a very young Sammy's makeup urges him to stay close to you wherever you go. Forcing a very young puppy to operate against his natural instincts can be bewildering.

The "Down" Command

Once your Samoyed has mastered the "sit" and "stay" commands, you may begin work on "down." This is the single word command for lie down. Use the "down" command only when you want the dog to lie down. If you want your dog to get off your sofa or to stop jumping up on people use the "off" command. Do not interchange these two commands. Doing so will only serve to confuse your dog and evoking the right response will become next to impossible.

The "down" position is especially useful if you want your Sammy to remain in a particular place for a long period of time.

A dog is usually far more inclined to stay put when he is lying down than when he is sitting.

Teaching this command to your Sammy may take more time and patience than the previous lessons. It is believed by some animal behaviorists that assuming the "down" position somehow represents submissiveness to the dog.

With your Sammy sitting in front of and facing you, hold a treat in your right hand with the excess part of the leash in your left hand. Hold the treat under the dog's nose and slowly bring your hand down to the ground. Your dog will follow the treat with his head and neck. As he does, give the command "down" and exert light pressure on the dog's shoulders with your left hand. If your dog resists the pressure on his shoulders do not continue pushing down, doing so will only create more resistance.

An alternative method of getting your Sammy headed into the down position is to move around to the dog's right side and as you draw his attention downward with your right hand, slide your left arm under the dog's front legs and gently slide them forward. In the case of a small puppy you will undoubtedly have to be on your knees next to the youngster.

As your Sammy's forelegs begin to slide out to its front, keep moving the treat along the ground until the dog's whole body is lying on the ground while you continually repeat "down." Once your Samoyed has assumed the position you desire, give him the treat and a lot of praise. Continue assisting your dog into the "down" position until he does so on his own. Be firm and be patient.

Barron's Blithe Spirit, UD, HT, OA disappears through the collapsed tunnel obstacle on an agility course.

The "Heel" Command

In learning to heel, your Sammy will walk on your left side with his shoulder next to your leg no matter which direction you might go or how quickly you turn. Teaching your Sammy to heel will not only make your daily walks far more enjoyable, it will make a far more tractable companion when the two of you are in crowded or confusing situations.

There are few breeds that are able to top the Samoyed in obedience. Barron's White Lighting, a top obedience champion, demonstrates the breed's ability by clearing the high jump.

Hand signals used in conjunction with verbal commands can be very effective. Ch. Tarahill's Treasure Me Always demonstrates her down/stay.

We have found a lightweight, link-chain training collar is very useful for the heeling lesson. It provides both quick

pressure around the neck and a snapping sound, both of which get the dog's attention. Erroneously referred to as a "choke collar," the link-chain collar used properly does not choke the dog. The pet shop at which you purchase the training collar will be able to show you the proper way to put this collar on your dog. Do not leave this collar on your puppy when training sessions are finished.

As you train your puppy to walk along on the leash, you should accustom the youngster to walk on your left side. The leash should cross your body from the dog's collar to your right hand. The excess portion of the leash will be folded into your right hand and your left hand on the leash will be used to make corrections with the leash.

Backpacking is just one event in which the versatile Samoyed can excel. These two Sammys illustrate proper placement and balance of their backpacks.

A quick short jerk on the leash with your left hand will keep your dog from lunging side to side, pulling ahead or lagging back. As you make a correction give the "heel" command. Keep the leash slack as long as your dog maintains the proper position at your side.

If your dog begins to drift away give the leash a sharp jerk and guide the dog back to the correct position and give the "heel" command. Do not pull on the lead with steady pressure. What is needed is a sharp but gentle jerking motion to get your dog's attention.

TRAINING CLASSES

There are few limits to what a patient, consistent Samoyed owner can teach his or her dog. For advanced obedience work beyond the basics it is wise for the Sammy owner to

Your Samoyed must be properly trained to participate in obedience or conformation events.

Training classes are an excellent way to begin teaching your Samoyed basic obedience. These classmates demonstrate the long sit.

consider local professional assistance. Professional trainers have had long standing experience in avoiding the pitfalls of obedience training and can help you to avoid these mistakes as well.

This training assistance can be obtained in many ways. Classes are particularly good for your Sammy's socialization and attentiveness. The dog will learn that it must obey even when there are other dogs and people around that provide temptation to run off and play. There are free-of-charge classes at many parks and recreation facilities, as well as very formal and sometimes very expensive individual lessons with private trainers.

There are also some obedience schools that will take your Sammy and train it for you. However, unless your schedule provides no time at all to train your own dog, having someone else train the dog for you would be last on our list of recommendations. The rapport that develops between the owner who has trained his or her Samoyed to be a pleasant companion and good canine citizen is very special—well worth the time and patience it requires to achieve.

VERSATILITY

The Samoyed is undoubtedly one of the most versatile breeds of dog known to man. Your Sammy will do anything you ask of it insolong as it is within his power to do so. A Samoyed may do what you ask in his own particular way but you can rely on the fact that a Sammy will give the command its all.

In leading reindeer herds across the trackless tundra and in defending the herds against predatory animals, the Samoyed is said to perform tasks beyond the wisdom and endurance of any other breed. The breed of course is used as a sled dog but they do equally well as herding dogs, weight pullers, packing dogs, tracking dogs and they are used more and more frequently as therapy dogs for the ill, aged and young

This Samoyed flies over the agility bar jump with the grace and agility that characterize the breed.

children. There are Samoyeds currently providing service assistance to their wheelchair-dependent owners.

Samoyeds have attained all levels of conformation and obedience titles. How far your Sammy goes in obedience work depends only on the level of your commitment and the time you have available. Your Samoyed will never let you down but because of the breed's keen sense of humor, be prepared to be embarrassed on occasion (especially those times when it is extra important that everything be done "just right"). Your Sammy will find many ways to turn obedience work into his or her own sort of game. Always be patient and bring your sense of humor along too!

SPORT of Purebred Dogs

by Judy Iby

Welcome to the exciting and sometimes frustrating sport of dogs. No doubt you are trying to learn more about dogs or you wouldn't be deep into this book. This section covers the basics that may entice you, further your knowledge and help you to understand the dog world. If you decide to give showing, obedience or any other dog activities a try, then I suggest you seek further help from the appropriate source.

Dog showing has been a very popular sport for a long time and has been taken quite seriously by some. Others only enjoy it as a hobby.

The Kennel Club in England was formed in 1859, the American Kennel Club was established in 1884 and the Canadian Kennel Club was formed in 1888. The purpose of these clubs was to register purebred dogs and maintain their Stud Books. In the beginning, the concept of registering dogs was not readily accepted. More than 36 million dogs have been enrolled in the AKC Stud Book since its inception in 1888. Presently the kennel clubs not only register dogs but adopt and enforce rules and regulations governing dog shows, obedience trials and field trials. Over the years they have fostered and encouraged interest in the health and welfare of the purebred

Conformation is just one of the many events in which you and your Sammy can compete.

dog. They routinely donate funds to veterinary research for study on genetic disorders.

Below are the addresses of the kennel clubs in the United States, Great Britain and Canada.

The American Kennel Club
51 Madison Avenue
New York, NY 10010
(Their registry is located at: 5580 Centerview Drive, STE 200, Raleigh, NC 27606-3390)

The Kennel Club
1 Clarges Street
Piccadilly, London, WIY 8AB, England

The Canadian Kennel Club
111 Eglinton Avenue
East Toronto, Ontario M6S 4V7
Canada

Your Sammy pup will need your discipline and guidance to become a well-mannered companion.

Today there are numerous activities that are enjoyable for both the dog and the handler. Some of the activities include conformation showing, obedience competition, tracking, agility, the Canine Good Citizen Certificate, and a wide range of instinct tests that vary from breed to breed. Where you start depends upon your goals which early on may not be readily apparent.

PUPPY KINDERGARTEN

Every puppy will benefit from this class. PKT is the foundation for all future dog activities from conformation to "couch potatoes." Pet owners should make an effort to attend even if they never expect to show their dog. The class is designed for puppies about three months of age with graduation at approximately five months of age. All the puppies will be in the same age group and, even though some may be a little unruly, there should not be any real problem. This class will teach the puppy some beginning obedience. As in all obedience classes the owner learns how to train his own dog. The PKT class gives the puppy the opportunity to interact with other puppies in the same age group and exposes him to strangers, which is very important. Some dogs grow up with behavior problems, one of them being fear of strangers. As you can see, there can be much to gain from this class.

Ch. Tega's Emerald City Rose owned by Gail and Terry Campbell.

There are some basic obedience exercises that every dog should learn. Some of these can be started with puppy kindergarten.

CONFORMATION

Conformation showing is our oldest dog show sport. This type of showing is based on the dog's appearance—that is his structure, movement and attitude. When considering this type of showing, you need to be aware of your breed's standard and be able to evaluate your dog compared to that standard. The breeder of your puppy or other experienced breeders would be good sources for such an evaluation. Puppies can go through lots of changes over a period of time. I always say most puppies start out as promising hopefuls and then after maturing may be disappointing as show candidates. Even so this should not deter them from being excellent pets.

Usually conformation training classes are offered by the local kennel or obedience clubs. These are excellent places for training puppies. The puppy should be able to walk on a lead before entering such a class. Proper ring procedure and technique for posing (stacking) the dog will be demonstrated as well as gaiting the dog. Usually certain patterns are used in the ring such as the triangle or the "L." Conformation class, like the PKT class, will give your youngster the opportunity to socialize with different breeds of dogs and humans too.

It takes some time to learn the routine of conformation showing. Usually one starts at the puppy matches which may be AKC Sanctioned or Fun Matches. These matches are generally for puppies from two or three months to a year old, and there may be classes for the adult over the age of 12 months. Similar to point shows, the classes are divided by sex and after completion of the classes in that breed or variety, the class winners compete for Best of Breed or Variety. The winner goes on to compete in the Group and the Group winners

compete for Best in Match. No championship points are awarded for match wins.

A few matches can be great training for puppies even though there is no intention to go on showing. Matches enable the puppy to meet new people and be handled by a stranger—the judge. It is also a change of environment, which broadens the horizon for both dog and handler. Matches and other dog activities boost the confidence of the handler and especially the younger handlers.

Earning an AKC championship is built on a point system, which is different from Great Britain. To become an AKC Champion of Record the dog must earn 15 points. The number of points earned each time depends upon the number of dogs in competition. The number of points available at each show depends upon the breed, its sex and the location of the show. The United States is divided into ten AKC zones. Each zone has its own set of points. The purpose of the zones is to try to equalize the points available from breed to breed and area to area. The AKC adjusts the point scale annually.

The number of points that can be won at a show are between one and five. Three-, four- and five-point wins are considered majors. Not only does the dog need 15 points won under three different judges, but those points must include two majors under two different judges. Canada also works on a point system but majors are not required.

Dogs always show before bitches. The classes available to those seeking points are: Puppy (which may be divided into 6 to 9 months and 9 to 12 months); 12 to 18 months; Novice; Bred-by-Exhibitor; American-bred; and Open. The class winners of the same sex of each breed or variety compete against each other for Winners Dog and Winners Bitch. A

Reserve Winners Dog and Reserve Winners Bitch are also awarded but do not carry any points

All Samoyeds can benefit from early training to teach them basic obedience.

Successful showing requires dedication and preparation, but most of all, it should be an enjoyable experience for both dog and owner.

unless the Winners win is disallowed by AKC. The Winners Dog and Bitch compete with the specials (those dogs that have attained championship) for Best of Breed or Variety, Best of Winners and Best of Opposite Sex. It is possible to pick up an extra point or even a major if the points are higher for the defeated winner than those of Best of Winners. The latter would get the higher total from the defeated winner.

At an all-breed show, each Best of Breed or Variety winner will go on to his respective Group and then the Group winners will compete against each other for Best in Show. There are seven Groups: Sporting, Hounds, Working, Terriers, Toys, Non-Sporting and Herding. Obviously there are no Groups at speciality shows (those shows that have only one breed or a show such as the American Spaniel Club's Flushing Spaniel Show, which is for all flushing spaniel breeds).

Earning a championship in England is somewhat different since they do not have a point system. Challenge Certificates are awarded if the judge feels the dog is deserving regardless of the number of dogs in competition. A dog must earn three

Challenge Certificates under three different judges, with at least one of these Certificates being won after the age of 12 months. Competition is very strong and entries may be higher than they are in the U.S. The Kennel Club's Challenge Certificates are only available at Championship Shows.

In England, The Kennel Club regulations require that certain dogs, Border Collies and Gundog breeds, qualify in a working capacity (i.e., obedience or field trials) before becoming a full Champion. If they do not qualify in the working aspect, then they are designated a Show Champion, which is equivalent to the AKC's Champion of Record. A Gundog may be granted the title of Field Trial Champion (FT Ch.) if it passes all the tests in the field but would also have to qualify in conformation before becoming a full Champion. A Border Collie that earns the title of Obedience Champion (Ob Ch.) must also qualify in the conformation ring before becoming a Champion.

The U.S. doesn't have a designation full Champion but does award for Dual and Triple Champions. The Dual Champion must be a Champion of Record, and either Champion Tracker, Herding Champion, Obedience Trial Champion or Field Champion. Any dog that has been awarded the titles of Champion of Record, and any two of the following: Champion Tracker, Herding Champion, Obedience Trial Champion or Field Champion, may be designated as a Triple Champion.

The shows in England seem to put more emphasis on breeder judges than those in the U.S. There is much competition within the breeds. Therefore the quality of the individual breeds should be very good. In the United States we tend to have more "all around judges" (those that judge multiple breeds) and use the breeder judges at the specialty shows. Breeder judges are more familiar with their own breed since they are actively breeding that breed or did so at one time. Americans emphasize Group and Best in Show wins and promote them accordingly.

It is my understanding that the shows in England can be very large and extend over several days, with the Groups being scheduled on different days. I believe there is only one all-breed show in the U.S. that extends over two days, the Westminster Kennel Club Show. In our country we have cluster shows, where several different clubs will use the same show site over consecutive days.

Westminster Kennel Club is our most prestigious show although the entry is limited to 2500. In recent years, entry has been limited to Champions. This show is more formal than the majority of the shows with the judges wearing formal attire and the handlers fashionably dressed. In most instances the quality of the dogs is superb. After all, it is a show of Champions. It is a good show to study the AKC registered breeds and is by far the most exciting—especially since it is televised! WKC is one of the few shows in this country that is still benched. This means the dog must be in his benched area during the show hours except when he is being groomed, in the ring, or being exercised.

Typically, the handlers are very particular about their appearances. They are careful not to wear something that will detract from their dog but will perhaps enhance it. American ring procedure is quite formal compared to that of other countries.

Agility is an action-packed sport that is quickly gaining in popularity.

I remember being reprimanded by a judge because I made a suggestion to a friend holding my second dog outside the ring. I certainly could have used more discretion so I would not call attention to myself. There is a certain etiquette expected between the judge and exhibitor and among the other exhibitors. Of course it is not always the case but the judge is supposed to be polite, not engaging in small talk or even acknowledging that he knows the handler. I understand that there is a more informal and relaxed atmosphere at the shows in other countries. For instance, the dress code is more casual. I can see where this might be more fun for the exhibitor and especially for the novice. This country is very handler-oriented in many of the breeds. It is true, in most instances, that the experienced professional handler can present the dog better and will have a feel for what a judge likes.

In England, Crufts is The Kennel Club's own show and is most assuredly the largest dog show in the world. They've been known to have an entry of nearly 20,000, and the show lasts four days. Entry is only gained by qualifying through winning in specified classes at another Championship Show. Westminster is strictly conformation, but Crufts exhibitors and spectators enjoy not only conformation but obedience, agility and a multitude of exhibitions as well. Obedience was admitted in 1957 and agility in 1983.

A Samoyed that competes in conformation must be perfectly groomed for presentation in the show ring.

If you are handling your own dog, please give some consideration to your apparel. For sure the dress code at matches is more informal than the point shows. However, you should wear something a little more appropriate than beach attire or ragged jeans and bare feet. If you check out the handlers and see what is presently fashionable, you'll catch on. Men usually dress with a shirt and tie and a nice sports coat. Whether you are male or female, you will want to wear comfortable clothes and shoes. You need to be able to run with your dog and you certainly don't want to take a chance of falling and hurting yourself. Heaven forbid, if nothing else, you'll upset your dog. Women usually wear a dress or two-piece outfit, preferably with pockets to carry bait, comb, brush, etc. In this case men are the lucky ones with all their pockets. Ladies, think about where your dress will be if you need to kneel on the floor and also think about running. Does it allow freedom to do so?

Years ago, after toting around all the baby paraphernalia, I found toting the dog and necessities a breeze. You need to take along dog; crate; ex pen (if you use one); extra newspaper; water pail and water; all required grooming equipment, including hair dryer and extension cord; table; chair for you; bait for dog and lunch for you and friends; and, last but not least, clean up materials, such as plastic bags, paper towels, and perhaps a bath towel and some shampoo—just in case. Don't forget your entry confirmation and directions to the show.

Terry Campbell is pictured winning with Ch. Tega's Izzy Ozzy's Pride.

If you are showing in obedience, then

you will want to wear pants. Many of our top obedience handlers wear pants that are color-coordinated with their dogs. The philosophy is that imperfections in the black dog will be less obvious next to your black pants.

Whether you are showing in conformation, Junior Showmanship or obedience, you need to watch the clock and be sure you are not late. It is customary to pick up your conformation armband a few minutes before the start of the class. They will not wait for you and if you are on the show grounds and not in the ring, you will upset everyone. It's a little more complicated picking up your obedience armband if you show later in the class. If you have not picked up your armband and they get to your number, you may not be allowed to show. It's best to pick up your armband early, but then you may show earlier than expected if other handlers don't pick up. Customarily all conflicts should be discussed with the judge prior to the start of the class.

Barron's Heather Blossom, NA manipulates the teeter totter with ease.

Junior Showmanship

The Junior Showmanship Class is a wonderful way to build self confidence even if there are no aspirations of staying with the dog-show game later in life. Frequently, Junior Showmanship becomes the background of those who become successful exhibitors/handlers in the future. In some instances it is taken very seriously, and success is measured in terms of wins. The Junior Handler is judged solely on his ability and skill in presenting his dog. The dog's conformation is not to be considered by the judge. Even so the condition and grooming of the dog may be a reflection upon the handler.

Usually the matches and point shows include different classes. The Junior Handler's dog may be entered in a breed or obedience class and even shown by another person in that class. Junior Showmanship classes are usually divided by age and perhaps sex. The age is determined by the handler's age on the day of the show.

The time you spend training your Samoyed will result in a close bond between dog and owner.

Canine Good Citizen

The AKC sponsors a program to encourage dog owners to train their dogs. Local clubs perform the pass/fail tests, and dogs who pass are awarded a Canine Good Citizen Certificate. Proof of vaccination is required at the time of participation. The test includes:

1. Accepting a friendly stranger.
2. Sitting politely for petting.
3. Appearance and grooming.
4. Walking on a loose leash.
5. Walking through a crowd.
6. Sit and down on command/staying in place.
7. Come when called.
8. Reaction to another dog.
9. Reactions to distractions.
10. Supervised separation.

If more effort was made by pet owners to accomplish these exercises, fewer dogs would be cast off to the humane shelter.

OBEDIENCE

Obedience is necessary, without a doubt, but it can also become a wonderful hobby or even an obsession. In my opinion, obedience classes and competition can provide wonderful companionship, not only with your dog but with your classmates or fellow competitors. It is always gratifying to discuss your dog's problems with others who have had similar experiences. The AKC acknowledged Obedience around 1936, and it has changed tremendously even though many of the exercises are basically the same. Today, obedience competition is just that—very competitive. Even so, it is possible for every obedience exhibitor to come home a winner (by earning qualifying scores) even though he/she may not earn a placement in the class.

Most of the obedience titles are awarded after earning three qualifying scores (legs) in the appropriate class under three different judges. These classes offer a perfect score of 200, which is extremely rare. Each of the class exercises has its own point value. A leg is earned after receiving a score of at least 170 and at least 50 percent of the points available in each exercise. The titles are:

Companion Dog–CD
This is called the Novice Class and the exercises are:

1. Heel on leash and figure 8	40 points
2. Stand for examination	30 points
3. Heel free	40 points
4. Recall	30 points
5. Long sit—one minute	30 points
6. Long down—three minutes	30 points
Maximum total score	200 points

Companion Dog Excellent–CDX
This is the Open Class and the exercises are:

1. Heel off leash and figure 8	40 points
2. Drop on recall	30 points
3. Retrieve on flat	20 points
4. Retrieve over high jump	30 points

5. Broad jump   20 points
6. Long sit–three minutes (out of sight)   30 points
7. Long down–five minutes (out of sight)   30 points
Maximum total score   200 points

Utility Dog–UD
The Utility Class exercises are:
1. Signal Exercise   40 points
2. Scent discrimination-Article 1   30 points
3. Scent discrimination-Article 2   30 points
4. Directed retrieve   30 points
5. Moving stand and examination   30 points
6. Directed jumping   40 points
Maximum total score   200 points

Sammys can do anything–including swim! These two youngsters contemplate taking a dip in the family swimming pool.

After achieving the UD title, you may feel inclined to go after the UDX and/or OTCh. The UDX (Utility Dog Excellent) title went into effect in January 1994. It is not easily attained. The title requires qualifying

simultaneously ten times in Open B and Utility B but not necessarily at consecutive shows.

The OTCh (Obedience Trial Champion) is awarded after the dog has earned his UD and then goes on to earn 100 championship points, a first place in Utility, a first place in Open and another first place in either class. The placements must be won under three different judges at all-breed obedience trials. The points are determined by the number of dogs competing in the Open B and Utility B classes. The OTCh title precedes the dog's name.

Obedience matches (AKC Sanctioned, Fun, and Show and Go) are usually available. Usually they are sponsored by the local obedience clubs. When preparing an obedience dog for a title, you will find matches very helpful. Fun Matches and Show and Go Matches are more lenient in allowing you to make corrections in the ring. I frequently train (correct) in the ring and inform the judge that I would like to do so and to please mark me "exhibition." This means that I will not be eligible for any prize. This type of training is usually very necessary for the Open and Utility Classes. AKC Sanctioned Obedience Matches do not allow corrections in the ring since they

Samoyeds throw themselves into competitions like the weight pull with great gusto.

Samoyeds excel at agility because of their natural dexterity and athleticism.

must abide by the AKC Obedience Regulations. If you are interested in showing in obedience, then you should contact the AKC for a copy of the Obedience Regulations.

TRACKING

Tracking is officially classified obedience, but I feel it should have its own category. There are three tracking titles available: Tracking Dog (TD), Tracking Dog Excellent (TDX), Variable Surface Tracking (VST). If all three tracking titles are obtained, then the dog officially becomes a CT (Champion Tracker). The CT will go in front of the dog's name.

A TD may be earned anytime and does not have to follow the other obedience titles. There are many exhibitors that prefer tracking to obedience, and there are others like myself that do both. In my experience with small dogs, I prefer to earn the CD and CDX before attempting tracking. My reasoning is that small dogs are closer to the mat in the obedience rings and therefore it's too easy to put the nose down and sniff. Tracking encourages sniffing. Of course this depends on the dog. I've had some dogs that tracked around the ring and others (TDXs) who wouldn't think of sniffing in the ring.

AGILITY

Agility was first introduced by John Varley in England at the Crufts Dog Show, February 1978, but Peter Meanwell, competitor and judge, actually developed the idea. It was officially recognized in the early '80s. Agility is extremely popular in England and Canada and growing in popularity in the U.S. The AKC acknowledged agility in August 1994. Dogs must be at least 12 months of age to be entered. It is a fascinating sport that the dog, handler and spectators enjoy to the utmost. Agility is a spectator sport! The dog performs off lead. The handler either runs with his dog or positions himself on the course and directs his dog with verbal and hand signals over a timed course over or through a variety of obstacles including a time out or pause. One of the main drawbacks to agility is finding a place to train. The obstacles take up a lot of space and it is very time consuming to put up and take down courses.

Agility is an exciting event for both the dog and the spectators. This Sammy conquers the tire jump with ease.

The titles earned at AKC agility trials are Novice Agility Dog (NAD), Open Agility Dog (OAD), Agility Dog Excellent (ADX), and Master Agility Excellent (MAX). In order to acquire an agility title, a dog must earn a qualifying score in its respective class on three separate occasions under two different judges. The MAX will be awarded after earning ten qualifying scores in the Agility Excellent Class.

PERFORMANCE TESTS

During the last decade the American Kennel Club has promoted performance tests— those events that test the different breeds' natural

This Samoyed shows his prowess and balance on the agility cat walk.

abilities. This type of event encourages a handler to devote even more time to his dog and retain the natural instincts of his breed heritage. It is an important part of the wonderful world of dogs.

Herding Titles
For all Herding breeds and Rottweilers and Samoyeds.

Entrants must be at least nine months of age and dogs with limited registration (ILP) are eligible. The Herding program is divided into Testing and Trial sections. The goal is to demonstrate proficiency in herding livestock in diverse situations. The titles offered are Herding Started (HS), Herding Intermediate (HI), and Herding Excellent (HX). Upon completion of the HX a Herding Championship may be earned after accumulating 15 championship points.

The above information has been taken from the AKC Guidelines for the appropriate events.

SCHUTZHUND
The German word "Schutzhund" translated to English means "Protection Dog." It is a fast growing competitive sport in the United States and has been popular in England since the early 1900s. Schutzhund was originally a test to determine which German Shepherds were quality dogs for breeding in Germany. It gives us the ability to test our dogs for correct temperament and working ability. Like every other dog sport, it requires teamwork between the handler and the dog.

Schutzhund training and showing involves three phases: Tracking, Obedience and Protection. There are three SchH levels: SchH I (novice), SchH II (intermediate), and SchH III

An exercise pen is just one of the pieces of equipment you may need when at a dog show.

(advanced). Each title becomes progressively more difficult. The handler and dog start out in each phase with 100 points. Points are deducted as errors are incurred. A total perfect score is 300, and for a dog and handler to earn a title he must earn at least 70 points in tracking and obedience and at least 80 points in protection. Today many different breeds participate successfully in Schutzhund.

A Sammy will try anything once! Ch. Barron's Heather Blossom, NA tackles the A-frame in an agility trial.

GENERAL INFORMATION

Obedience, tracking and agility allow the purebred dog with an Indefinite Listing Privilege (ILP) number or a limited registration to be exhibited and earn titles. Application must be made to the AKC for an ILP number.

The American Kennel Club publishes a monthly *Events* magazine that is part of the *Gazette*, their official journal for the sport of purebred dogs. The *Events* section lists upcoming shows and the secretary or superintendent for them. The majority of the conformation shows in the U.S. are overseen by licensed superintendents. Generally the entry closing date is approximately two-and-a-half weeks before the actual show. Point shows are fairly expensive, while the match shows cost about one third of the point show entry fee. Match shows usually take entries the day of the show but some are pre-entry. The best way to find match show information is through your local kennel club. Upon asking, the AKC can provide you with a list of superintendents, and you can write and ask to be put on their mailing lists.

Obedience trial and tracking test information is available through the AKC. Frequently these events are not superintended, but put on by the host club. Therefore you would make the entry with the event's secretary.

As you have read, there are numerous activities you can share with your dog. Regardless what you do, it does take teamwork. Your dog can only benefit from your attention and training. I hope this chapter has enlightened you and hope, if nothing else, you will attend a show here and there. Perhaps you will start with a puppy kindergarten class, and who knows where it may lead!

HEALTH CARE

by Judy Iby

Veterinary medicine has become far more sophisticated than what was available to our ancestors. This can be attributed to the increase in household pets and consequently the demand for better care for them. Also human medicine has become far more complex. Today diagnostic testing in veterinary medicine parallels human diagnostics. Because of better technology we can expect our pets to live healthier lives thereby increasing their life spans.

Preventive health care throughout your Samoyed's life will result in a happier and healthier pet.

THE FIRST CHECK UP

You will want to take your new puppy/dog in for its first check up within 48 to 72 hours after acquiring it. Many breeders strongly recommend this check up and so do the humane shelters. A puppy/dog can appear healthy but it may have a serious problem that is not apparent to the layman. Most pets have some type of a minor flaw that may never cause a real problem.

Unfortunately if he/she should have a serious problem, you will want to consider the consequences of keeping the pet and the attachments that will be formed, which may be broken prematurely. Keep in mind there are many healthy dogs looking for good homes.

This first check up is a good time to establish yourself with the veterinarian and learn the office policy regarding their hours and how they handle emergencies. Usually the breeder or another conscientious pet owner is a good reference for locating a capable veterinarian. You should be aware that not all veterinarians give the same quality of service. Please do not make your selection on the least expensive clinic, as they may be short changing your pet. There is the possibility that eventually it will cost you more due to improper diagnosis, treatment, etc. If you are selecting a new veterinarian, feel free to ask for a tour of the clinic. You should inquire about making

an appointment for a tour since all clinics are working clinics, and therefore may not be available all day for sightseers. You may worry less if you see where your pet will be spending the day if he ever needs to be hospitalized.

THE PHYSICAL EXAM

Your veterinarian will check your pet's overall condition, which includes listening to the heart; checking the respiration; feeling the abdomen, muscles and joints; checking the mouth, which includes the gum color and signs of gum disease along with plaque buildup; checking the ears for signs of an infection or ear mites; examining the eyes; and, last but not least, checking the condition of the skin and coat.

He should ask you questions regarding your pet's eating and elimination habits and invite you to relay your questions. It is a good idea to prepare a list so as not to forget anything. He should discuss the proper diet and the quantity to be fed. If this should differ from your breeder's recommendation, then you should convey to him the breeder's choice and see if he approves. If he recommends changing the diet, then this should be done over a few days so as not to cause a gastrointestinal upset. It is customary to take in a fresh stool sample (just a small amount) for a test for intestinal parasites. It must be fresh, preferably within 12 hours, since the eggs hatch quickly and after hatching will not be observed under the microscope. If your pet isn't obliging then, usually the technician can take one in the clinic.

IMMUNIZATIONS

It is important that you take your puppy/dog's vaccination record with you on your first visit. In case of a puppy,

A regular physical exam will ensure your Samoyed's good health and improve the quality of his life.

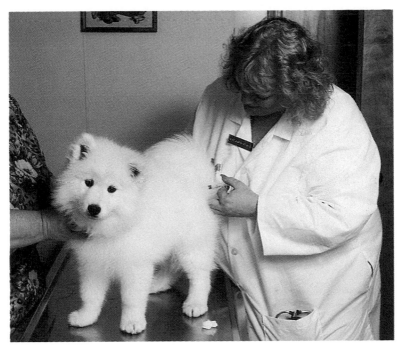

Immunizations will protect your vulnerable Samoyed pup from many life-threatening diseases.

presumably the breeder has seen to the vaccinations up to the time you acquired custody. Veterinarians differ in their vaccination protocol. It is not unusual for your puppy to have received vaccinations for distemper, hepatitis, leptospirosis, parvovirus and parainfluenza every two to three weeks from the age of five or six weeks. Usually this is a combined injection and is typically called the DHLPP. The DHLPP is given through at least 12 to 14 weeks of age, and it is customary to continue with another parvovirus vaccine at 16 to 18 weeks. You may wonder why so many immunizations are necessary. No one knows for sure when the puppy's maternal antibodies are gone, although it is customarily accepted that distemper antibodies are gone by 12 weeks. Usually parvovirus antibodies are gone by 16 to 18 weeks of age. However, it is possible for the maternal antibodies to be gone at a much earlier age or even a later age. Therefore immunizations are started at an early age. The vaccine will not give immunity as long as there are maternal antibodies.

109

The rabies vaccination is given at three or six months of age depending on your local laws. A vaccine for bordetella (kennel cough) is advisable and can be given anytime from the age of five weeks. The coronavirus is not commonly given unless there is a problem locally. The Lyme vaccine is necessary in endemic areas. Lyme disease has been reported in 47 states.

Distemper

This is virtually an incurable disease. If the dog recovers, he is subject to severe nervous disorders. The virus attacks every tissue in the body and resembles a bad cold with a fever. It can cause a runny nose and eyes and cause gastrointestinal disorders, including a poor appetite, vomiting and diarrhea. The virus is carried by raccoons, foxes, wolves, mink and other dogs. Unvaccinated youngsters and senior citizens are very susceptible. This is still a common disease.

Hepatitis

This is a virus that is most serious in very young dogs. It is spread by contact with an infected animal or its stool or urine. The virus affects the liver and kidneys and is characterized by high fever, depression and lack of appetite. Recovered animals may be afflicted with chronic illnesses.

Leptospirosis

This is a bacterial disease transmitted by contact with the urine of an infected dog, rat or other wildlife. It produces severe symptoms of fever, depression, jaundice and internal bleeding and was fatal before the vaccine was developed.

Dogs can pick up diseases from other dogs, so make sure your Sammy pup is properly vaccinated before taking him out to make friends.

Recovered dogs can be carriers, and the disease can be transmitted from dogs to humans.

Parvovirus

This was first noted in the late 1970s and is still a fatal disease. However, with proper vaccinations, early diagnosis and prompt treatment, it is a manageable disease. It attacks the bone marrow and intestinal tract. The

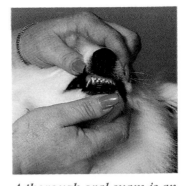

A thorough oral exam is an important part of your Samoyed's regular check-up.

Once you bring your Sammy pup home, he will depend on you to take care of his health and well being.

symptoms include depression, loss of appetite, vomiting, diarrhea and collapse. Immediate medical attention is of the essence.

Rabies

This is shed in the saliva and is carried by raccoons, skunks, foxes, other dogs and cats. It attacks nerve tissue, resulting in paralysis and death. Rabies can be transmitted to people and is virtually always fatal. This disease is reappearing in the suburbs.

Bordetella (Kennel Cough)

The symptoms are coughing, sneezing, hacking and retching accompanied by nasal discharge usually lasting from a few days to several weeks. There are several disease-producing organisms responsible for this disease. The present vaccines are helpful but do not protect for all the strains. It usually is not life threatening but in some instances it can progress to a serious bronchopneumonia. The disease is highly contagious. The vaccination should be given routinely for dogs that come in contact with other dogs, such as through boarding, training class or visits to the groomer.

Coronavirus

This is usually self limiting and not life threatening. It was first noted in the late '70s about a year before parvovirus. The virus produces a yellow/brown stool and there may be depression, vomiting and diarrhea.

Lyme Disease

This was first diagnosed in the United States in 1976 in Lyme, CT in people who lived in close proximity to the deer tick. Symptoms may include acute lameness, fever, swelling of

Bordetella attached to canine cilia. Otherwise known as kennel cough, this disease is very contagious and should be vaccinated against routinely.

joints and loss of appetite. Your veterinarian can advise you if you live in an endemic area.

After your puppy has completed his puppy vaccinations, you will continue to booster the DHLPP once a year. It is customary to booster the rabies one year after the first vaccine and then, depending on where you live, it should be boostered every year or every three years. This depends on your local laws. The Lyme and corona vaccines are boostered annually and it is recommended that the bordetella be boostered every six to eight months.

The deer tick is the most common carrier of Lyme disease. Photo courtesy of Virbac Laboratories, Inc., Fort Worth, Texas.

ANNUAL VISIT

I would like to impress the importance of the annual check up, which would include the booster vaccinations, check for intestinal parasites and test for heartworm. Today in our very busy world it is rush, rush and see "how much you can get for how little." Unbelievably, some non-veterinary businesses have entered into the vaccination business. More harm than good can come to your dog through improper vaccinations, possibly from inferior vaccines and/or the wrong schedule. More than likely you truly care about your companion dog and over the years you have devoted much time and expense to his well being. Perhaps you are unaware that a vaccination is not just a vaccination. There is more involved. Please, please follow through with regular physical examinations. It is so important for your veterinarian to know your dog and this is especially true during middle age through the geriatric years. More than likely your older dog will require more than one physical a year. The annual physical is good preventive medicine. Through early diagnosis and subsequent treatment your dog can maintain a longer and better quality of life.

INTESTINAL PARASITES

Hookworms

These are almost microscopic intestinal worms that can

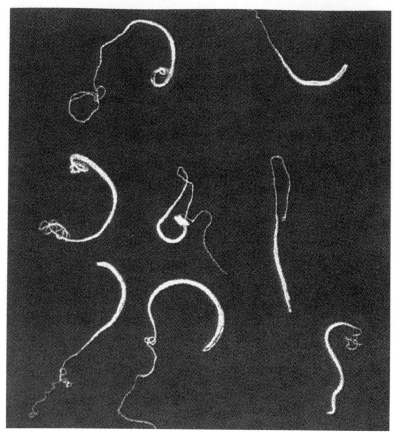

Whipworms are difficult to find and it is a job best left to a veterinarian. Pictured here are adult whipworms.

cause anemia and therefore serious problems, including death, in young puppies. Hookworms can be transmitted to humans through penetration of the skin. Puppies may be born with them.

Roundworms

These are spaghetti-like worms that can cause a potbellied appearance and dull coat along with more severe symptoms, such as vomiting, diarrhea and coughing. Puppies acquire these while in the mother's uterus and through lactation. Both hookworms and roundworms may be acquired through ingestion.

Whipworms

These have a three-month life cycle and are not acquired through the dam. They cause intermittent diarrhea usually with mucus. Whipworms are possibly the most difficult worm to eradicate. Their eggs are very resistant to most environmental factors and can last for years until the proper conditions enable them to mature. Whipworms are seldom seen in the stool.

Intestinal parasites are more prevalent in some areas than others. Climate, soil and contamination are big factors contributing to the incidence of intestinal parasites. Eggs are passed in the stool, lay on the ground and then become infective in a certain number of days. Each of the above worms has a different life cycle. Your best chance of becoming and remaining worm-free is to always pooper-scoop your yard. A fenced-in yard keeps stray dogs out, which is certainly helpful.

Roundworm eggs, as seen on a fecal evaluation. The eggs must develop for at least 12 days before they are infective.

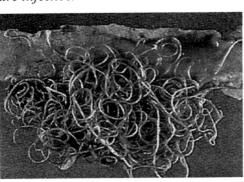

I would recommend having a fecal examination on your dog twice a year or more often if there is a problem. If your dog has a positive fecal sample, then he will be given the appropriate medication and you will be asked to bring back another stool sample in a certain period of time (depending on the type of worm) and then be rewormed. This process goes on until he has at least two negative samples. The different types of worms require different medications. You will be wasting your money and doing your dog an injustice by buying over-the-counter medication without first consulting your veterinarian.

OTHER INTERNAL PARASITES

Coccidiosis and Giardiasis

These protozoal infections usually affect puppies, especially in places where large numbers of puppies are brought together. Older dogs may harbor these infections but do not show signs unless they are stressed. Symptoms include diarrhea, weight loss and lack of appetite. These infections are not always apparent in the fecal examination.

Tapeworms

Seldom apparent on fecal floatation, they are diagnosed frequently as rice-like segments around the dog's anus and the base of the tail. Tapeworms are long, flat and ribbon like, sometimes several feet in length, and made up of many segments about five-eighths of an inch long. The two most common types of tapeworms found in the dog are:

(1) First the larval form of the flea tapeworm parasite must mature in an intermediate host, the flea, before it can become infective. Your dog acquires this by ingesting the flea through licking and chewing.

(2) Rabbits, rodents and certain

Your Samoyed can pick up parasites like fleas and ticks when outdoors. Make sure to check his coat thoroughly after playing outside.

large game animals serve as intermediate hosts for other species of tapeworms. If your dog should eat one of these infected hosts, then he can acquire tapeworms.

HEARTWORM DISEASE

This is a worm that resides in the heart and adjacent blood vessels of the lung that produces microfilaria, which circulate in the bloodstream. It is possible for a dog to be infected with any number of worms from one to a hundred that can be 6 to 14 inches long. It is a life-threatening disease, expensive to treat and easily prevented. Depending on where you live, your veterinarian may recommend a preventive year-round and either an annual or semiannual blood test. The most common preventive is given once a month.

The cat flea is the most common flea of both dogs and cats. It starts feeding soon after it makes contact with the animal.

EXTERNAL PARASITES

Fleas

These pests are not only the dog's worst enemy but also enemy to the owner's pocketbook. Preventing is less expensive than treating, but regardless I think we'd prefer to spend our money elsewhere. I would guess that the majority of our dogs are allergic to the bite of a flea, and in many cases it only takes one flea bite. The protein in the flea's saliva is the culprit. Allergic dogs have a reaction, which usually results in a "hot spot." More than likely such a reaction will involve a trip to the veterinarian for treatment. Yes, prevention is less expensive. Fortunately today there are several good products available.

If there is a flea infestation, no one product is going to correct the problem. Not only will the dog require treatment so will the environment. In general flea collars are not very effective although there is now available an "egg" collar that will kill the eggs on the dog. Dips are the most economical but they are messy. There are some effective shampoos and treatments available through pet shops and veterinarians. An oral tablet arrived on the American market in 1995 and was popular in Europe the previous year. It sterilizes the female flea but will not kill adult fleas. Therefore the tablet, which is given monthly, will decrease the flea population but is not a "cure-all." Those dogs that suffer from flea-bite allergy will still be subjected to the bite of the flea. Another popular parasiticide is permethrin, which is applied to the back of the dog in one or two places depending on the dog's weight. This product works as a repellent causing the flea to get "hot feet" and jump off. Do not confuse this product with some of the organophosphates that are also applied to the dog's back.

By breeding only the best quality dogs, good health and temperament is passed down to each generation.

Some products are not usable on young puppies. Treating fleas should be done under your veterinarian's guidance. Frequently it is necessary to combine products and the layman does not have the knowledge regarding possible toxicities. It is hard to believe but there are a few dogs that do have a natural resistance to fleas. Nevertheless it would be wise to treat all pets at the same time. Don't forget your cats. Cats just love to prowl the neighborhood and consequently return with unwanted guests.

Adult fleas live on the dog but their eggs drop off the dog into the environment. There they go through four larval stages before reaching adulthood, and thereby are able to jump back on the poor unsuspecting dog. The cycle resumes and takes between 21 to 28 days under ideal conditions. There are environmental products available that will kill both the adult fleas and the larvae.

Ticks

Ticks carry Rocky Mountain Spotted Fever, Lyme disease and can cause tick paralysis. They should be removed with tweezers, trying to pull out the head. The jaws carry disease. There is a tick preventive collar that does an excellent job. The ticks automatically back out on those dogs wearing collars.

Sarcoptic Mange

This is a mite that is difficult to find on skin scrapings. The

pinnal reflex is a good indicator of this disease. Rub the ends of the pinna (ear) together and the dog will start scratching with his foot. Sarcoptes are highly contagious to other dogs and to humans although they do not live long on humans. They cause intense itching.

Demodectic Mange

This is a mite that is passed from the dam to her puppies. It affects youngsters age three to ten months. Diagnosis is confirmed by skin scraping. Small areas of alopecia around the eyes, lips and/or forelegs become visible. There is little itching unless there is a secondary bacterial infection. Some breeds are afflicted more than others.

Cheyletiella

This causes intense itching and is diagnosed by skin scraping. It lives in the outer layers of the skin of dogs, cats, rabbits and humans. Yellow-gray scales may be found on the back and the rump, top of the head and the nose.

TO BREED OR NOT TO BREED

More than likely your breeder has requested that you have your puppy neutered or spayed. Your breeder's request is based on what is healthiest for your dog and what is most beneficial for your breed. Experienced and conscientious breeders devote many years into developing a bloodline. In order to do this, he makes every effort to plan each breeding in regard to conformation, temperament and health. This type of

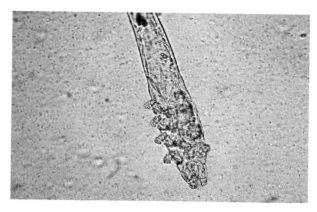

The demodex mite is passed from the dam to her puppies. It affects youngsters from the ages of three to ten months.

breeder does his best to perform the necessary testing (i.e., OFA, CERF, testing for inherited blood disorders, thyroid, etc.). Testing is expensive and sometimes very disheartening when a favorite dog doesn't pass his health tests. The health history pertains not only to the breeding stock but to the immediate ancestors. Reputable breeders do not want their offspring to be bred indis-

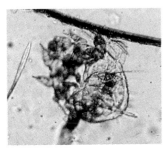

Sarcoptes are highly contagious to other dogs and to humans, and can cause intense itching.

A healthy Samoyed will be able to accomplish anything he sets his mind to.

criminately. Therefore you may be asked to neuter or spay your puppy. Of course there is always the exception, and your breeder may agree to let you breed your dog under his

direct supervision. This is an important concept. More and more effort is being made to breed healthier dogs.

Spay/Neuter

There are numerous benefits of performing this surgery at six months of age. Unspayed females are subject to mammary and ovarian cancer. In order to prevent mammary cancer she must be spayed prior to her first heat cycle. Later in life, an unspayed female may develop a pyometra (an infected uterus), which is definitely life threatening.

Spaying/neutering is often the best option for your family pet. It minimizes the risk of certain diseases and helps prevent unwanted litters.

Spaying is performed under a general anesthetic and is easy on the young dog. As you might expect it is a little harder on the older dog, but that is no reason to deny her the surgery. The surgery removes the ovaries and uterus. It is important to remove all the ovarian tissue. If some is left behind, she could remain attractive to males. In order to view the ovaries, a reasonably long incision is necessary. An ovariohysterectomy is considered major surgery.

Neutering the male at a young age will inhibit some characteristic male behavior that owners frown upon. I have found my boys will not hike their legs and mark territory if they are neutered at six months of age. Also neutering at a young age has hormonal benefits, lessening the chance of hormonal aggressiveness.

Surgery involves removing the testicles but leaving the scrotum. If there should be a retained testicle, then he definitely needs to be neutered before the age of two or three years. Retained testicles can develop into cancer. Unneutered males are at risk for testicular cancer, perineal fistulas, perianal tumors and fistulas and prostatic disease.

Provide your Samoyed pup with the proper health care—he'll thank you for it!

Intact males and females are prone to housebreaking accidents. Females urinate frequently before, during and after heat cycles, and males tend to mark territory if there is a female in heat. Males may show the same behavior if there is a visiting dog or guests.

Surgery involves a sterile operating procedure equivalent to human surgery. The incision site is shaved, surgically scrubbed and draped. The veterinarian wears a sterile surgical gown, cap, mask and gloves. Anesthesia should be monitored by a registered technician. It is customary for the veterinarian to recommend a pre-anesthetic blood screening, looking for metabolic problems and a ECG rhythm strip to check for normal heart function. Today anesthetics are equal to human anesthetics, which enables your dog to walk out of the clinic the same day as surgery.

Some folks worry about their dog gaining weight after being neutered or spayed. This is usually not the case. It is true that some dogs may be less active so they could develop a problem, but my own dogs are just as active as they were before surgery. I have a hard time keeping weight on them. However, if your dog should begin to gain, then you need to decrease his food and see to it that he gets a little more exercise.

MEDICAL PROBLEMS

Anal Sacs

These are small sacs on either side of the rectum that can cause the dog discomfort when they are full. They should empty when the dog has a bowel movement. Symptoms of inflammation or impaction are excessive licking under the tail and/or a bloody or sticky discharge from the anal area. Breeders like myself recommend emptying the sacs on a regular schedule when bathing the dog. Many veterinarians prefer this isn't done unless there are symptoms. You can express the sacs by squeezing the two sacs (at the five and seven o'clock positions) in and up toward the anus. Take precautions not to get in the way of the foul-smelling fluid that is expressed. Some dogs object to this procedure so it would be wise to have someone hold the head. Scooting is caused by anal-sac irritation and not worms.

Colitis

The stool may be frank blood or blood tinged and is the result of inflammation of the colon. Colitis, sometimes intermittent, can be the result of stress, undiagnosed whipworms, or perhaps idiopathic (no explainable reason). I have had several dogs prone to this disorder. They felt fine and were willing to eat but would have intermittent bloody stools. If this in an ongoing problem, you should probably feed a diet higher in fiber. Seek professional help if your dog feels poorly and/or the condition persists.

Conjunctivitis

Many breeds are prone to this problem. The conjunctiva is the pink tissue that lines the inner surface of the eyeball except the clear, transparent cornea. Irritating substances such as bacteria, foreign matter or chemicals can cause it to become reddened and swollen. It is important to keep any hair trimmed from around the eyes. Long hair stays damp and aggravates the problem. Keep the eyes cleaned with warm water and wipe away any matter that has accumulated in the corner of the eyes. If the condition persists, you should see your veterinarian. This problem goes hand in hand with keratoconjunctivitis sicca.

Your Samoyed's eyes should be clear and free of redness or irritation.

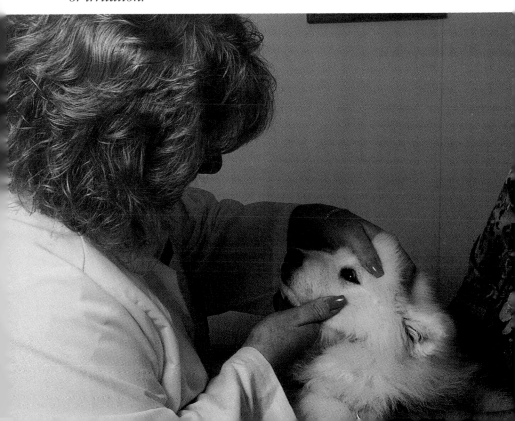

DENTAL CARE for Your Dog's Life

So you've got a new puppy! You also have a new set of puppy teeth in your household. Anyone who has ever raised a puppy is abundantly aware of these new teeth. Your puppy will chew anything it can reach, chase your shoelaces, and play "tear the rag" with any piece of clothing it can find. When puppies are newly born, they have no teeth. At about four weeks of age, puppies of most breeds begin to develop their deciduous or baby teeth. They begin eating semi-solid food, fighting and biting with their litter mates, and learning discipline from their mother. As their new teeth come in, they inflict more pain on their

Make sure your Samoyed has a safe Nylabone® to play with to satisfy his chewing needs.

there are calculus deposits below the gum line, the veterinarian will plane the roots to make them smooth. After all of the calculus has been removed, the teeth are polished with pumice in a polishing cup. If any medical or surgical treatment is needed, it is done at this time. The final step would be fluoride treatment and your follow-up treatment at home. If the periodontal disease is advanced, the veterinarian may prescribe a medicated mouth rinse or antibiotics for use at home. Make sure your dog has safe, clean and attractive chew toys and treats. Chooz® treats are another way of using a consumable treat to help keep your dog's teeth clean.

Rawhide is the most popular of all materials for a dog to chew. This has never been good news to dog owners, because rawhide is inherently very dangerous for dogs. Thousands of dogs have died from rawhide, having swallowed the hide after it has become soft and mushy, only to cause stomach and intestinal blockage. A new rawhide product on the market has finally solved the problem of rawhide: molded Roar-Hide® from Nylabone. These are composed of processed, cut up, and melted American rawhide injected into your dog's favorite shape: a dog bone. These dog-safe devices smell and taste like

Roar-Hide™ is completely edible, high in protein (over 86%) and low in fat (less than one-third of 1%). Unlike common rawhide, it is safer, less messy and more fun for your Samoyed!

The CarrotBone™ by Nylabone® is a durable chew containing no plastics or artificial ingredients, and it can be served as is, in bone-hard form, or microwaved to a biscuity consistency.

rawhide but don't break up. The ridges on the bones help to fight tartar build-up on the teeth and they last ten times longer than the usual rawhide chews.

As your dog ages, professional examination and cleaning should become more frequent. The mouth should be inspected at least once a year. Your veterinarian may recommend visits every six months. In the geriatric patient, organs such as the heart, liver, and kidneys do not function as well as when they were young. Your veterinarian will probably want to test these organs' functions prior to using general anesthesia for dental cleaning. If your dog is a good chewer and you work closely with your veterinarian, your dog can keep all of its teeth all of its life. However, as your dog ages, his sense of smell, sight, and taste will diminish. He may not have the desire to chase, trap or chew his toys. He will also not have the energy to chew for long periods, as arthritis and periodontal disease make chewing painful. This will leave you with more responsibility for keeping his teeth clean and healthy. The dog that would not let you brush his teeth at one year of age, may let you brush his teeth now that he is ten years old.

If you train your dog with good chewing habits as a puppy, he will have healthier teeth throughout his life.

TRAVELING with Your Dog

by Judy Iby

The earlier you start traveling with your new puppy or dog, the better. He needs to become accustomed to traveling. However, some dogs are nervous riders and become carsick easily. It is helpful if he starts with an empty stomach. Do not despair, as it will go better if you continue taking him with you on short fun rides. How would you feel if every time you rode in the car you stopped at the doctor's for an injection? You would soon dread that nasty car. Older dogs that tend to get carsick may have more of a problem adjusting to traveling. Those dogs that are having a serious problem may benefit from some medication prescribed by the veterinarian.

The well-trained and well-socialized Samoyed is a suitable traveling companion— and can even carry his own luggage!

Do give your dog a chance to relieve himself before getting into the car. It is a good idea to be prepared for a clean up with a leash, paper towels, bag and terry cloth towel.

The safest place for your dog is in a fiberglass crate, although close confinement can promote carsickness in some dogs. If your dog is nervous you can try letting him ride on the seat next to you or in someone's lap.

Crates are the safest way for your dog to travel in the car.

An alternative to the crate would be to use a car harness made for dogs and/or a safety strap attached to the harness or collar. Whatever you do, do not let your dog ride in the back of a pickup truck unless he is securely tied on a very short lead. I've seen trucks stop quickly and, even though the dog was tied, it fell out and was dragged.

I do occasionally let my dogs ride loose with me because I really enjoy their companionship, but in all honesty they are safer in their crates. I have a friend whose van rolled in an accident but his dogs, in their fiberglass crates, were not injured nor did they escape. Another advantage of the crate is that it is a safe place to leave him if you need to run into the store. Otherwise you wouldn't be able to leave the windows down. Keep in mind that while many dogs are overly protective in their crates, this may not be enough to deter dognappers. In some states it is against the law to leave a dog in the car unattended.

Never leave a dog loose in the car wearing a collar and leash. I have known more than one dog that has killed himself by hanging. Do not let him put his head out an open window. Foreign debris can be blown into his eyes. When leaving your dog unattended in a car, consider the temperature. It can take less than five minutes to reach temperatures over 100 degrees Fahrenheit.

TRIPS

Perhaps you are taking a trip. Give consideration to what is best for your dog—traveling with you or boarding. When traveling by car, van or motor home, you need to think ahead about locking your vehicle. In all probability you have many valuables in the car and do not wish to leave it unlocked.

Perhaps most valuable and not replaceable is your dog. Give thought to securing your vehicle and providing adequate ventilation for him. Another consideration for you when traveling with your dog is medical problems that may arise and little inconveniences, such as exposure to external parasites. Some areas of the country are quite flea infested. You may want to carry flea spray with you. This is even a good idea when staying in motels. Quite possibly you are not the only occupant of the room.

Can we come too? These Sammys look ready to follow their owner anywhere.

Unbelievably many motels and even hotels do allow canine guests, even some very first-class ones. Gaines Pet Foods Corporation publishes *Touring With Towser*, a directory of domestic hotels and motels that accommodate guests with dogs. Their address is Gaines TWT, PO Box 5700, Kankakee, IL, 60902. I would recommend you call ahead to any motel that you may be considering and see if they accept pets. Sometimes it is necessary to pay a deposit against room damage. Of course you are more likely to gain accommodations for a small dog than a large dog. Also the management feels reassured when you mention that your dog will be crated. Since my dogs tend to bark when I leave the room, I leave the TV on nearly full blast to deaden the noises outside that tend to encourage my dogs to bark. If you do travel with your dog, take along plenty of baggies so that you can clean up after him. When we all do our share in cleaning up, we make it possible for motels to continue accepting our pets. As a matter of fact, you should practice cleaning up everywhere you take your dog.

Depending on where your are traveling, you may need an up-to-date health certificate issued by your veterinarian. It is good policy to take along your dog's medical information, which would include the name, address and phone number of your veterinarian, vaccination record, rabies certificate, and any medication he is taking.

Because he is so versatile and accommodating, the Samoyed fares well in any climate and on any kind of vacation.

Air Travel

When traveling by air, you need to

contact the airlines to check their policy. Usually you have to make arrangements up to a couple of weeks in advance for traveling with your dog. The airlines require your dog to travel in an airline approved fiberglass crate. Usually these can be purchased through the airlines but they are also readily available in most pet-supply stores. If your dog is not accustomed to a crate, then it is a good idea to get him acclimated to it before your trip. The day of the actual trip you should withhold water about one hour ahead of departure and no food for about 12 hours. The airlines generally have temperature restrictions, which do not allow pets to travel if it is either too cold or too hot. Frequently these restrictions are based on the temperatures at the departure and arrival airports. It's best to inquire about a health certificate. These usually need to be issued within ten days of departure. You should arrange for non-stop, direct flights and if a commuter plane should be involved, check to see if it will carry dogs. Some don't. The Humane Society of the United States has put together a tip sheet for airline traveling. You can receive a copy by sending a self-addressed stamped envelope to:

The Humane Society of the United States
Tip Sheet
2100 L Street NW
Washington, DC 20037.

Regulations differ for traveling outside of the country and are sometimes changed without notice. Well in advance you need to write or call the appropriate consulate or agricultural department for instructions. Some countries have lengthy quarantines (six months), and countries differ in their rabies vaccination requirements. For instance, it may have to be given at least 30 days ahead of your departure.

Do make sure your dog is wearing proper identification. You never know when you might be in an accident and separated from your dog. Or your dog could be frightened and somehow manage to escape and run away. When I travel, my dogs wear collars with engraved nameplates with my name, phone number and city.

Another suggestion would be to carry in-case-of-emergency instructions. These would include the address and phone number of a relative or friend, your veterinarian's name, address and phone number, and your dog's medical information.

BOARDING KENNELS

Perhaps you have decided that you need to board your dog. Your veterinarian can recommend a good boarding facility or possibly a pet sitter that will come to your house. It is customary for the boarding kennel to ask for proof of vaccination for the DHLPP, rabies and bordetella vaccine. The bordetella should have been given within six months of boarding. This is for your protection. If they do not ask for this proof I would not board at their kennel. Ask about flea control. Those dogs that suffer flea-bite allergy can get in trouble at a boarding kennel. Unfortunately boarding kennels are limited on how much they are able to do.

For more information on pet sitting, contact NAPPS:
National Association of Professional Pet Sitters
1200 G Street, NW
Suite 760
Washington, DC 20005.

Our clinic has technicians that pet sit and technicians that board clinic patients in their homes. This may be an alternative for you. Ask your veterinarian if they have an employee that can help you. There is a definite advantage of having a technician care for your dog, especially if your dog is on medication or is a senior citizen.

You may consider boarding your Samoyed in a reputable kennel if you go away.

You can write for a copy of *Traveling With Your Pet* from ASPCA, Education Department, 441 E. 92nd Street, New York, NY 10128.

IDENTIFICATION and Finding the Lost Dog

by Judy Iby

Where are several ways of identifying your dog. The old standby is a collar with dog license, rabies, and ID tags. Unfortunately collars have a way of being separated from the dog and tags fall off. I am not suggesting you shouldn't use a collar and tags. If they stay intact and on the dog, they are the quickest way of identification.

For several years owners have been tattooing their dogs. Some tattoos use a number with a registry. Here lies the problem because there are several registries to check. If you wish to tattoo,

Always keep your Samoyed on a leash to keep him from becoming separated from you.

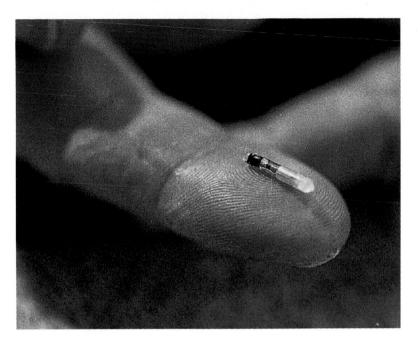

The newest method of identification is the microchipping. The microchip is a computer chip that is no bigger than a grain of rice.

use your social security number. The humane shelters have the means to trace it. It is usually done on the inside of the rear thigh. The area is first shaved and numbed. There is no pain, although a few dogs do not like the buzzing sound. Occasionally tattooing is not legible and needs to be redone.

The newest method of identification is microchipping. The microchip is a computer chip that is no larger than a grain of rice. The veterinarian implants it by injection between the shoulder blades. The dog feels no discomfort. If your dog is lost and picked up by the humane society, they can trace you by scanning the microchip, which has its own code. Microchip scanners are friendly to other brands of microchips and their registries. The microchip comes with a dog tag saying the dog is microchipped. It is the safest way of identifying your dog.

FINDING THE LOST DOG

I am sure you will agree with me that there would be little worse than losing your dog. Responsible pet owners rarely lose their dogs. They do not let their dogs run free because they don't want harm to come to them. Not only that but in most, if not all, states there is a leash law.

Beware of fenced-in yards. They can be a hazard. Dogs find ways to escape either over or under the fence. Another fast exit is through the gate that perhaps the neighbor's child left unlocked.

Below is a list that hopefully will be of help to you if you need it. Remember don't give up, keep looking. Your dog is worth your efforts.

Because the Samoyed is an independent breed, a secure, fenced-in yard is essential in order to keep him from wandering off.

1. Contact your neighbors and put flyers with a photo on it in their mailboxes. Information you should include would be the dog's name, breed, sex, color, age, source of identification, when your dog was last seen and where, and your name and phone numbers. It may be helpful to say the dog needs medical care. Offer a *reward*.
2. Check all local shelters daily. It is also possible for your dog to be picked up away from home and end up in an out-of-the-way shelter. Check these too. Go in person. It is not good enough to call. Most shelters are limited on the time they can hold dogs then they are put up for adoption or euthanized. There is the possibility that your dog will not make it to the shelter for several days. Your dog could have been wandering or someone may have tried to keep him.
3. Notify all local veterinarians. Call and send flyers.
4. Call your breeder. Frequently breeders are contacted when one of their breed is found.
5. Contact the rescue group for your breed.
6. Contact local schools—children may have seen your dog.
7. Post flyers at the schools, groceries, gas stations, convenience stores, veterinary clinics, groomers and any other place that will allow them.
8. Advertise in the newspaper.
9. Advertise on the radio.

BEHAVIOR and Canine Communication

by Judy Iby

Studies of the human/animal bond point out the importance of the unique relationships that exist between people and their pets. Those of us who share our lives with pets understand the special part they play through companionship, service and protection. For many, the pet/owner bond goes beyond simple companionship; pets are often considered members of the family. A leading pet food manufacturer recently conducted a nationwide survey of pet owners to gauge just how important pets were in their lives. Here's what they found:

• 76 percent allow their pets to sleep on their beds

Although some traits are inherited within a breed, every Samoyed is an individual with his own personality.

• 78 percent think of their pets as their children
• 84 percent display photos of their pets react to their own emotions

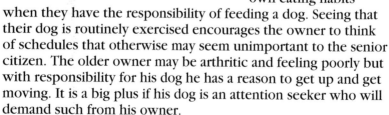

• 100 percent talk to their pets
• 97 percent think that their pets understand what they're saying

Are you surprised?

Senior citizens show more concern for their own eating habits when they have the responsibility of feeding a dog. Seeing that their dog is routinely exercised encourages the owner to think of schedules that otherwise may seem unimportant to the senior citizen. The older owner may be arthritic and feeling poorly but with responsibility for his dog he has a reason to get up and get moving. It is a big plus if his dog is an attention seeker who will demand such from his owner.

Over the last couple of decades, it has been shown that pets relieve the stress of those who lead busy lives. Owning a pet has been known to lessen the occurrence of heart attack and stroke.

Dogs are very important parts of their owner's life and the bond between humans and animals is a strong one.

Many single folks thrive on the companionship of a dog. Lifestyles are very different from a long time ago, and today more individuals seek the single life. However, they receive fulfillment from owning a dog.

Most likely the majority of our dogs live in family environments. The companionship they provide is well worth the effort involved. In my opinion, every child should have the opportunity to have a family dog. Dogs teach responsibility through understanding their care, feelings and even respecting their life cycles. Frequently those children who have not been exposed to dogs grow up afraid of dogs, which isn't good. Dogs sense timidity and some will take advantage of the situation.

Today more dogs are serving as service dogs. Since the origination of the Seeing Eye dogs years ago, we now have

trained hearing dogs. Also dogs are trained to provide service for the handicapped and are able to perform many different tasks for their owners. Search and Rescue dogs, with their handlers, are sent throughout the world to assist in recovery of disaster victims. They are life savers.

Therapy dogs are very popular with nursing homes, and some hospitals even allow them to visit. The inhabitants truly look forward to their visits. I have taken a couple of my dogs visiting and left in tears when I saw the response of the patients. They wanted and were allowed to have my dogs in their beds to hold and love.

Because boredom can lead to mischief in dogs, make sure your Sammy has plenty of toys to play with and gets enough exercise.

Nationally there is a Pet Awareness Week to educate students and others about the value and basic care of our pets. Many countries take an even greater interest in their pets than Americans do. In those countries the pets are allowed to accompany their owners into restaurants and shops, etc. In the U.S. this freedom is only available to our service dogs. Even so we think very highly of the human/animal bond.

CANINE BEHAVIOR

Canine behavior problems are the number-one reason for pet owners to dispose of their dogs, either through new homes, humane shelters or euthanasia. Unfortunately there are too many owners who are unwilling to devote the necessary time to properly train their dogs. On the other hand, there are those who not only are concerned about inherited health problems but are also aware of the dog's mental stability.

Ch. Suruka J Yuru, owned by Donald and Dot Hodges, is an excellent example of both a quality show dog and beloved family pet.

You may realize that a breed and his group relatives (i.e., sporting, hounds, etc.) show tendencies to behavioral characteristics. An experienced breeder can acquaint you with his breed's personality. Unfortunately many breeds are labeled with poor temperaments when actually the breed as a whole is not affected but only a small percentage of individuals within the breed.

If the breed in question is very popular, then of course there may be a higher number of unstable dogs. Do not label a breed good or bad. I know of absolutely awful-tempered dogs within one of our most popular, lovable breeds.

Inheritance and environment contribute to the dog's behavior. Some naïve people suggest inbreeding as the cause of bad temperaments. Inbreeding only results in poor behavior if the ancestors carry the trait. If there are excellent temperaments behind the dogs, then inbreeding will promote good temperaments in the offspring. Did you ever consider that inbreeding is what sets the characteristics of a breed? A purebred dog is the end result of inbreeding. This does not spare the mixed-breed dog from the same problems. Mixed-breed dogs frequently are the offspring of purebred dogs.

When planning a breeding, I like to observe the potential stud and his offspring in the show ring. If I see unruly behavior, I try to look into it further. I want to know if it is genetic or environmental, due to the lack of training and socialization. A good breeder will avoid breeding mentally unsound dogs.

Not too many decades ago most of our dogs led a different lifestyle than what is prevalent today. Usually mom stayed home so the dog had human companionship and someone to discipline it if needed. Not much was expected from the dog. Today's mom works and everyone's life is at a much faster pace.

The dog may have to adjust to being a "weekend" dog. The family is gone all day during the week, and the dog is left to his own devices for entertainment. Some dogs sleep all day waiting for their family to come home and others become wigwam wreckers if given the opportunity. Crates do ensure the safety of the dog and the house. However, he could become a physically and emotionally cripple

As long as they are properly introduced, a well-socialized Samoyed will get along great with other pets. This Sammy and Dachshund make fast friends.

Does this look like the face of a troublemaker? Even sweethearts like this can get into trouble if not properly supervised.

if he doesn't get enough exercise and attention. We still appreciate and want the companionship of our dogs although we expect more from them. In many cases we tend to forget dogs are just that—*dogs* not human beings.

I own several dogs who are left crated during the day but I do try to make time for them in the evenings and on the weekends. Also we try to do something together before I leave for work. Maybe it helps them to have the companionship of other dogs. They accept their crates as their personal "houses" and seem to be content with their routine and thrive on trying their best to please me.

SOCIALIZING AND TRAINING

Many prospective puppy buyers lack experience regarding the proper socialization and training needed to develop the type of pet we all desire. In the first 18 months, training does take some work. Trust me, it is easier to start proper training before there is a problem that needs to be corrected.

The initial work begins with the breeder. The breeder should start socializing the puppy at five to six weeks of age and cannot let up. Human socializing is critical up through 12 weeks of age

The Samoyed is one of the most easy-going breeds in existence. These two pose for a Christmas portrait.

and likewise important during the following months. The litter should be left together during the first few weeks but it is necessary to separate them by ten weeks of age. Leaving them together after that time will increase competition for litter dominance. If puppies are not socialized with people by 12 weeks of age, they will be timid in later life.

The eight- to ten-week age period is a fearful time for puppies. They need to be handled very gently around children and adults. There should be no harsh discipline during this time. Starting at 14 weeks of age, the puppy begins the juvenile period, which ends when he reaches sexual maturity around six to 14 months of age. During the juvenile period he needs to be introduced to strangers (adults, children and other dogs) on the home property. At sexual maturity he will begin to bark at strangers and become more protective. Males start to lift their legs to urinate but if you desire you can inhibit this behavior by walking your boy on leash away from trees, shrubs, fences, etc.

Perhaps you are thinking about an older puppy. You need to inquire about the puppy's social experience. If he has lived in a kennel, he may have a hard time adjusting to people and environmental stimuli. Assuming he has had a good social upbringing, there are advantages to an older puppy.

Training includes puppy kindergarten and a minimum of one to two basic training classes. During these classes you will learn how to dominate your youngster. This is especially important if you own a large breed of dog. It is somewhat harder, if not nearly impossible, for some owners to be the Alpha figure when their dog towers over them. You will be taught how to properly restrain your dog. This concept is important. Again it puts you in the Alpha position. All dogs need to be restrained many times

Well-socialized pups should be able to play with each other without showing fear or aggression.

during their lives. Believe it or not, some of our worst offenders are the eight-week-old puppies that are brought to our clinic. They need to be gently restrained for a nail trim but the way they carry on you would think we were killing them. In comparison, their vaccination is a "piece of cake." When we ask dogs to do something that is not agreeable to them, then their worst comes out. Life will be easier for your dog if you expose him at a young age to the necessities of life—proper behavior and restraint.

UNDERSTANDING THE DOG'S LANGUAGE

Most authorities agree that the dog is a descendent of the wolf. The dog and wolf have similar traits. For instance both are pack oriented and prefer not to be isolated for long periods of time. Another characteristic is that the dog, like the wolf, looks to the leader—Alpha—for direction. Both the wolf and the dog communicate through body language, not only within their pack but with outsiders.

Every pack has an Alpha figure. The dog looks to you, or should look to you, to be that leader. If your dog doesn't receive the proper training and guidance, he very well may replace you as Alpha. This would be a serious problem and is certainly a disservice to your dog.

Eye contact is one way the Alpha wolf keeps order within his pack. You are Alpha so you must establish eye contact with your puppy. Obviously your puppy will have to look at you. Practice eye contact even if you need to hold his head for five to ten seconds at a time. You can give him a treat as a reward. Make sure your eye contact is gentle and not threatening. Later, if he has been naughty, it is permissible to give him a long, penetrating look. I caution you there are some older dogs that never learned eye contact as puppies and cannot accept eye contact. You should avoid eye contact with these dogs since they feel threatened and will retaliate as such.

BODY LANGUAGE

The play bow, when the forequarters are down and the hindquarters are elevated, is an invitation to play. Puppies play fight, which helps them learn the acceptable limits of biting. This is necessary for later in their lives. Nevertheless, an owner may be falsely reassured by the playful nature of his dog's aggression. Playful aggression toward another dog or human may be an indication

This Samoyed shows his submissive side— or perhaps he just wants a tummy rub!

of serious aggression in the future. Owners should never play fight or play tug-of-war with any dog that is inclined to be dominant.

Signs of submission are:

    1. Avoids eye contact.

    2. Active submission—the dog crouches down, ears back and the tail is lowered.

    3. Passive submission—the dog rolls on his side with his hindlegs in the air and frequently urinates.

Signs of dominance are:

This Sammy puppy uses body language to display his feelings—he is either very bored or very sleepy!

    1. Makes eye contact.

    2. Stands with ears up, tail up and the hair raised on his neck.

    3. Shows dominance over another dog by standing at right angles over it.

Dominant dogs tend to behave in characteristic ways such as:

    1. The dog may be unwilling to move from his place (i.e., reluctant to give up the sofa if the owner wants to sit there).

    2. He may not part with toys or objects in his mouth and may show possessiveness with his food bowl.

    3. He may not respond quickly to commands.

    4. He may be disagreeable for grooming and dislikes to be petted.

Dogs are popular because of their sociable nature. Those that have contact with humans during the first 12 weeks of life regard them as a member of their own species—their pack. All dogs have the potential for both dominant and submissive behavior. Only through experience and training do they learn to whom it is appropriate to show which behavior. Not all dogs are concerned with dominance but owners need to be aware of that potential. It is wise for the owner to establish his dominance early on.

A human can express dominance or submission toward a dog in the following ways:

    1. Meeting the dog's gaze signals dominance. Averting the gaze signals submission. If the dog growls or threatens, averting the gaze is the first avoiding action to take—it may

prevent attack. It is important to establish eye contact in the puppy. The older dog that has not been exposed to eye contact may see it as a threat and will not be willing to submit.

2. Being taller than the dog signals dominance; being lower signals submission. This is why, when attempting to make friends with a strange dog or catch the runaway, one should kneel down to his level. Some owners see their dogs become dominant when allowed on the furniture or on the bed. Then he is at the owner's level.

3. An owner can gain dominance by ignoring all the dog's social initiatives. The owner pays attention to the dog only when he obeys a command.

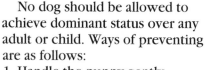

It is fine to give your Sammy the occasional treat, but make sure it does not interfere with his regular feeding times or food intake.

No dog should be allowed to achieve dominant status over any adult or child. Ways of preventing are as follows:

1. Handle the puppy gently, especially during the three- to four-month period.
2. Let the children and adults handfeed him and teach him to take food without lunging or grabbing.
3. Do not allow him to chase children or joggers.
4. Do not allow him to jump on people or mount their legs. Even females may be inclined to mount. It is not only a male habit.
5. Do not allow him to growl for any reason.
6. Don't participate in wrestling or tug-of-war games.
7. Don't physically punish puppies for aggressive behavior. Restrain him from repeating the infraction and teach an alternative behavior. Dogs should earn everything they receive from their owners. This would include sitting to receive petting or treats, sitting before going out the door and sitting to receive the collar and leash. These types of exercises reinforce the owner's dominance.

Young children should never be left alone with a dog. It is

Samoyeds are highly intelligent and trainable dogs whose capacity and ability know no bounds!

important that children learn some basic obedience commands so they have some control over the dog. They will gain the respect of their dog.

FEAR

One of the most common problems dogs experience is being fearful. Some dogs are more afraid than others. On the lesser side, which is sometimes humorous to watch, my dog can be afraid of a strange object. He acts silly when something is out of place in the house. I call his problem perceptive intelligence. He realizes the abnormal within his known environment. He does not react the same way in strange environments since he does not know what is normal.

On the more serious side is a fear of people. This can result in backing off, seeking his own space and saying "leave me alone" or it can result in an aggressive behavior that may lead to challenging the person. Respect that the dog wants to be left alone and give him time to come forward. If you approach the cornered dog, he may resort to snapping. If you leave him alone, he may decide to come forward, which should be rewarded with a treat. Years ago we had a dog that behaved in this manner. We coaxed people to stop by the house and make friends with our fearful dog. She learned to take the treats and after weeks of work she overcame her suspicions and made friends more readily.

Some dogs may initially be too fearful to take treats. In these cases it is helpful to make sure the dog hasn't eaten for about 24 hours. Being a little hungry encourages him to accept the treats, especially if they are of the "gourmet" variety. I have a dog that worries about strangers since people seldom stop by my house. Over the years she has learned a cue and jumps up quickly to visit anyone sitting on the sofa. She learned by herself that all guests on the sofa were to be trusted friends. I think she felt more comfortable with them being at her level, rather than towering over her.

Every dog deserves proper training in order to become a valued family member.

Dogs can be afraid of numerous things, including loud noises and thunderstorms. Invariably the owner rewards (by comforting) the dog when it shows signs of fearfulness. When your dog is frightened, direct his attention to something else and act happy. Don't dwell on his fright.

AGGRESSION

Some different types of aggression are: predatory, defensive, dominance, possessive, protective, fear induced, noise provoked, "rage" syndrome (unprovoked aggression), maternal and aggression directed toward other dogs. Aggression is the most common behavioral problem encountered. Protective breeds are expected to be more aggressive than others but with

the proper upbringing they can make very dependable companions. You need to be able to read your dog.

Many factors contribute to aggression including genetics and environment. An improper

A loaf of bread, a jug of wine and a Sammy? Dogs love "people" food, but this puppy is taking it too far!

environment, which may include the living conditions, lack of social life, excessive punishment, being attacked or frightened by an aggressive dog, etc., can all influence a dog's behavior. Even spoiling him and giving too much praise may be detrimental. Isolation and the lack of human contact or exposure to frequent teasing by children or adults also can ruin a good dog.

Lack of direction, fear, or confusion lead to aggression in those dogs that are so inclined. Any obedience exercise, even the sit and down, can direct the dog and overcome fear and/or confusion. Every dog should learn these commands as a youngster, and there should be periodic reinforcement.

When a dog is showing signs of aggression, you should speak calmly (no screaming or hysterics) and firmly give a command that he understands, such as the sit. As soon as your dog obeys, you have assumed your dominant position. Aggression presents a problem because there may be danger to others. Sometimes it is an emotional issue. Owners may consciously or unconsciously encourage their dog's aggression. Other owners show responsibility by accepting the problem and taking measures to keep it under control. The owner is responsible for his dog's actions, and it is not wise to take a chance on someone being bitten, especially a child. Euthanasia is the solution for some owners and in severe cases this may be the best choice. However, few dogs are that dangerous and very few are that much of a threat to their owners. If caution is exercised and professional help is gained early on, then I surmise most cases can be controlled.

Some authorities recommend feeding a lower protein (less than 20 percent) diet. They believe this can aid in reducing aggression. If the dog loses weight, then vegetable oil can be added. Veterinarians and behaviorists are having some success with pharmacology. In many cases treatment is possible and can improve the situation.

If you have done everything according to "the book" regarding training and socializing and are still having a behavior problem, don't procrastinate. It is important that the problem gets attention before it is out of hand. It is estimated that 20 percent of a veterinarian's time may be devoted to dealing with problems before they become so intolerable that the dog is separated from its home and owner. If your veterinarian isn't able to help, he should refer you to a behaviorist.

SUGGESTED READING

H-954
This is the Samoyed
Joan McDonald Brearly
384 pages, over 290 full
color photos.

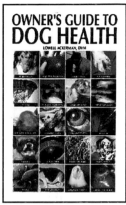

TS-214
Owner's Guide to Dog Health
Dr. Lowell Ackerman, DVM
432 pages, over 300
full color photos.

TS-257
Choosing A Dog For Life
Andrew DePrisco
384 pages,over 800 full
color photos.

TS-249
Skin and Coat Care For
Your Dog
Dr. Lowell Ackerman,
DVM
224 pages, over 190
full color photos.

INDEX